trotman

Law

UNCOVERED

trotman

Law

UNCOVERED

Margaret McAlpine

Law Uncovered
This first edition published in 2003 by Trotman and Company Ltd
2 The Green, Richmond, Surrey TW9 1PL

© Trotman and Company Limited 2003

Editorial and Publishing Team

Author Margaret McAlpine
Editorial Mina Patria, Editorial Director; Rachel Lockhart,
Commissioning Editor; Anya Wilson, Editor; Erin Milliken,
Editorial Assistant
Production Ken Ruskin, Head of Pre-press and Production
Sales and Marketing Deborah Jones, Head of Sales and
Marketing
Managing Director Toby Trotman

Designed by XAB

British Library Cataloguing in Publication Data
A catalogue record for this book is available
from the British Library

ISBN 0 85660 898 X

Typeset by Palimpsest Book Production Limited,
Polmont, Stirlingshire

Printed and bound in Great Britain by
Creative Print & Design Group (Wales) Ltd

*'The law is the true embodiment
of everything that's excellent.
It has no kind of fault or flaw
And I, my Lords, embody the Law.'*

(From *Iolanthe*, W.S. Gilbert and Arthur Sullivan)

CONTENTS

ABOUT THE AUTHOR

Margaret McAlpine taught for a number of years in schools and colleges in the Midlands and East Anglia, before becoming a journalist. Today she writes for a variety of publications and has a particular interest in writing careers materials for young people. Her other books published by Trotman include *What can I do with . . . a law degree?*, *What can I do with . . . a media studies degree?* and *What can I do with . . . no degree?*

She has three grown-up children and lives with her husband in Suffolk.

CHAPTER 1

Myths and facts –
A realistic look at a legal career

SO YOU'RE INTERESTED IN A LEGAL CAREER

Otherwise why would you have picked up this book?

Whether you're at school and considering education and training options, or are already in work but thinking, however vaguely, of a career change, something made you choose this book rather than one on information technology, aromatherapy or bee-keeping.

MAKING UP YOUR MIND

That's one thing this book will not do for you, and neither will any other book, so beware of one that suggests it could. You have to make your mind up for yourself and ignore people who think they can make a better job of it than you can.

What the following chapters aim to do is to help you to see a legal career for what it is – warts and all.

Law is one of those areas of work, like medicine, that seem to have instant appeal, and that can be dangerous. Immediate assumptions can be very misleading.

As a first step, take a moment to examine your views of different careers and measure them against reality.

THE MYTH

Law – prestigious, highly respectable, top salaries, long lunches, crisp white shirts and blouses.

Medicine – drama, heroism, saving lives, romantic hospital liaisons, grateful patients and loads of job satisfaction.

Teaching – long hours, little money, rude and difficult pupils, discipline problems, lunch duties in smelly dining halls plus hours of marking.

Retail – low pay, unsociable hours, limited promotion prospects, boring days on the shop floor organising deliveries and overseeing the stacking of tins of baked beans.

THE REALITY

Law – there are more highly paid areas of work, such as finance and some sectors of information technology. **The majority of lawyers earn moderate salaries and put in long hours.**

Medicine – as a doctor you're more likely to treat patients with infected toenails, strained backs and depression than you are to be performing surgery.

Teaching – the pay is not nearly as dire as it once was. There are strong incentives to enter the profession and for the right type of person, teaching is a rewarding career with excellent prospects.

Retail – the major national chains offer good training programmes and are keen to attract the right type of people with interesting packages and job opportunities.

WHERE DO YOUR IDEAS COME FROM?

Television has a great deal to answer for when it comes to stereotyping careers.

Legal and medical themes are top choices for TV dramas: *North Square*, *Kavanagh QC*, *LA Law*, *Ally McBeal* – not to mention *Casualty*, *Holby City* and *ER* in the medical sector – attract millions of viewers.

They show beautiful people tracking down villains and making sure that right prevails in between carrying out tempestuous affairs and eating in expensive restaurants. The wonder is that such characters have time to switch on their computers or prescribe an aspirin, let alone earn a living.

On the other hand, programmes set in schools or retail stores tend to be either knockabout comedies featuring inadequate nerds, or gritty dramas where head teachers suffer premature heart attacks chasing truants over school roofs.

A DOSE OF REALISM – A JOB IS A JOB

It takes up a great deal of precious time and, however prestigious or glamorous, all jobs contain periods of boredom and disillusion.

Even top politicians, shapers of the destiny of the world, spend time threading paper clips together and clicking on their emails in search of distraction. Famous actors rehearse in draughty halls and spend days on location in remote, wet, depressing places, nursing colds and sore throats and wishing they were back at home.

However, the need for realism doesn't mean that finding the right job isn't worth a lot of work and effort.

On average, you're going to spend something like 2,000 hours a year at work over a working life of at least 30 years, so it's worth finding a career that you enjoy, that uses your particular talents and gives you job satisfaction.

A CHANGE IS AS GOOD AS A REST

The attractions a career holds for you at 18 may be wearing thin at the age of 35. The days are largely gone when people went into their first job and stayed there for 40 years and then collected a gold watch and a pension, and spent their retirement digging their allotment.

Today an increasing number of people have at least one major career change during the course of their working lives, as their needs and interests change and develop.

Law does attract mature entrants and there is no reason why, with determination, it shouldn't be a fulfilling later career choice.

On leaving school Judy Banyard trained as a nursery nurse. She is now litigation manager in a firm of lawyers in the Midlands.

What does your job involve?
My firm specialises in preparing serious fraud cases for court administration work. I work as part of the defence team checking proof of evidence, going over papers and preparing reports and schedules.

I have my own legal caseload of matrimonial law, wills and probate cases. I also have general management duties and I'm in charge of IT systems.

What led you to a legal career?
I loved working with children, but when I took a career break to bring up my son and daughter I began to think about other options. I heard about a four-year part-time law degree that sounded really interesting and applied for a place.

Was it difficult to get a job?
After graduation I enrolled on the Legal Practice Course to

become a solicitor, but failed to qualify on the first attempt.
I could have retaken the course, but decided against it.

By that time I'd been offered a job with a legal firm, which
did not depend on passing the course, and took the job.

I opted for the Institute of Legal Executives training, where my
qualifications exempted me from all but two of the papers.

So you're not a solicitor?
No, but that doesn't stop me doing any of the work I enjoy.
Legal executives can now train as solicitors, so the old
difference between solicitors and legal executives is
disappearing.

STILL INTERESTED IN A LEGAL CAREER? THEN START HERE . . .

The term 'legal career' covers a massive range of jobs so the first
step is to narrow down your options.

You may be tempted to skip the section that follows because facing
questions to which you may have no answers can be confusing and
depressing and can make achieving your dreams seem light years
away.

However, you need to bear in mind the fact that legal training is
lengthy and expensive and before embarking on it you need some
sort of route map pointing you in a certain direction. That way you
may change direction, but you're less likely to find yourself wandering
around lost in a fog.

Simply wanting a legal career may be a good starting point, but
before committing yourself to education and training, a lot more
research is needed. So how about pondering on the questions
below:

● Do you see yourself as a barrister/advocate or a solicitor? (This
  is a major question so spend some time on it.)

- What area of law do you want to specialise in?

- Do you want to work in a particular region of the UK? Are you prepared to move to London?

- How are you going to finance your studies?

- Do you need to consider part-time courses that will allow you to earn some sort of income?

- Is earn-as-you-learn work-based training a more realistic option?

Once you start considering these questions, dozens more will rush into your head as you begin to flesh out what was once a vague idea into an achievable strategy and separate the fantasy from the reality.

TRY BEFORE YOU BUY

Once you have some ideas about the areas of legal work that might interest you, it's time to put them to the test.

There's only one way to find out if a job, any job, is right for you: try it and see.

Nobody in their right mind buys a house without viewing it, or purchases a car without taking it on a test drive. Finding the right career is more important than either of these activities and nobody should consider entering any profession without finding out for themselves what the work involves.

HOW DO I FIND WORK EXPERIENCE?

To start with you could pick up the phone and ask. This might sound drastic, but the direct approach is often the best.

If you're at school, college or university, careers teachers or careers officers are good points of contact and should have some useful advice and practical leads. Your local Connexions office could also prove helpful and the phone number will be in your local Yellow Pages.

Otherwise, personal contact is the way forward. You will find most people are helpful and are usually prepared to arrange for you to visit their premises, shadow a member of staff, or have a work experience placement with their firm. If this is not possible they should be able to give you the names of organisations or individuals who can help.

STILL NO IDEA WHERE YOU'RE GOING?

Good. That makes for a healthy start. Now read on. Spend a few hours learning a few facts about legal careers and what they might offer you. Then you should be in a better position to start making decisions.

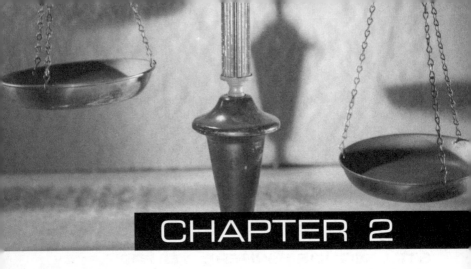

CHAPTER 2

What is law?
How has it developed?

Law is the set of rules by which a country is governed.

Living in a group or society brings with it rights and obligations. You behave in a certain way and with luck your pay-off is that other people will behave in the same way towards you and the rest of your group.

If people behaved exactly as they liked, with no consideration for others, there would be chaos, nobody would be safe and civilised society would collapse, which is why laws are required. They set out the rules of a society, how they should be put into practice and the penalties inflicted on people who break them.

THE BEGINNING

Laws were almost certainly in place long before they were written down. From earliest times we have lived in groups and have relied on each other for survival. While some members of a prehistoric clan went off to hunt, others stayed behind to protect the group, look after the old and the very young, prepare food and make weapons.

This interdependence brought strength to the group, but it was based on people accepting obligations. Some people might have wanted to take advantage of a hunter's absence to attack his family, steal his furs and move into his cave, but what stopped them was the knowledge that if they broke the laws of the group, they would be punished.

The probability is that these laws were based on custom, or what had gone before. A person is stoned to death for killing a member of the tribe. The next person to kill someone is treated in the same way and the pattern becomes established. Nothing is written down, but everyone knows more or less where they stand.

PUTTING IT IN WRITING

The invention of writing between about 3500 and 3000 BC meant laws could be recorded rather than remembered.

The first of such records appeared in the Middle East in Babylonia. The most famous Babylonian law code is that of King Hammurabi, which was drawn up in the 1700s BC. It covers issues ranging from adultery to theft and faulty workmanship in house building. Punishments were harsh and death or the loss of a limb was quite common.

THE WORD OF GOD

Around 1200 BC, the Israelites put their religious and social laws into a code, known as the Mosaic Code of Laws after the Israelite leader Moses.

According to the Old Testament, Moses was handed the section of these laws known as the Ten Commandments directly from God on tablets of stone. With the spread of Christianity, the Ten Commandments have had a great impact on the content of the law in Western civilisations.

THE GREEKS HAD A NAME FOR IT

Just as Moses was supposed to have received the Ten Commandments from God, most societies believed in some way that laws were made by the gods or goddesses they worshipped.

It was the Ancient Greeks who decided human beings were capable of setting up their own laws and changing them when necessary. Athens' first code of law was drawn up by Drako in 621 BC. Unfortunately, his punishments were so harsh that his name lives on in the word 'draconian', meaning extremely severe.

Luckily for the Athenians, around 80 years later a fairer code was drawn up followed by an increase in the law-making powers of the Athenian assembly.

ROMAN LAW

The Laws of the Twelve Tables was the first known Roman law code and Roman schoolboys had to learn it as part of their education. These laws remained the basis of Roman law, although the Romans adapted them to meet changing circumstances.

After 27 BC, the Roman Emperor was able to change laws as he wished, which led to major complications. The only people able to interpret the huge number of Roman laws were the *juris prudentes* or experts in law, In modern English the term jurisprudence means the science of law.

A number of rulers tried to organise Roman law into some kind of order and this was finally completed by the Emperor Justinian I. His code covered the whole area of law so efficiently that it became the basis for modern law codes and today the codes of many civil law countries are based on Roman law.

ALL GOOD THINGS COME TO AN END

In 395 BC the Roman Empire split into two: the East or Byzantine Empire with its capital in Constantinople (modern Istanbul), which escaped major invasions and where Roman law remained more or less intact. The West Roman Empire fell apart under attacks from Germanic invaders and most of the legal and cultural heritage of the Romans gradually died out. However, Roman law did survive

in the west as the basis for canon law – the law of the Roman
Catholic Church.

FEUDAL ALLEGIANCES

As civilisation collapsed in Western Europe, loyalties shrank to a
feudal level as populations looked to local lords to protect them.
People agreed to fight for their lord and in return he gave them
land and his armies defended their community against attacks
from outsiders.

THE GREAT DIVIDE

In mainland Europe commerce and industry began to thrive during
the 1000s, which brought with it a need for more complex laws
than those that suited life under the much simpler feudal systems.

Around 1100 the Italian university of Bologna started to train
students from Italy and neighbouring countries in Roman law.
Other universities followed their example and by the 1500s Roman
law had been adopted throughout most of mainland Europe.

VIVE LA FRANCE

In order to centralise their government and increase their power,
European kings tried hard to set up national legal codes for their
countries. In 1800 Napoleon Bonaparte set up a committee to
codify French civil law. The result was the Code Napoleon, which
was so successful that it remains France's basic legal code today
and became the model for civil law codes in most European
countries.

1066 AND ALL THAT

But not in England! This was because by the time mainland
Europe was developing Roman or civil law systems England had
already developed its own legal system.

William the Conqueror and his Norman army defeated the Saxons
at the Battle of Hastings and established a strong national
government. The Normans found a system of local courts in

operation across England. These were administering law on a local level with courts giving different judgments from area to area.

The Normans saw no reason to mend something that wasn't broken. They kept the system of local courts, but introduced the 'general eyre', by which representatives of the king were sent from Westminster to record details of land and wealth, collect taxes and give judgement in any disputes brought before them.

These representatives were known as itinerant justices and were the original royal judges. They were able to hear civil cases, which previously had to be heard in London. This meant cases were dealt with more speedily and efficiently compared to the local courts that were often corrupt and unfair.

(An ancient law allowed the inhabitants of Hereford to kill Welsh people on a Sunday as long as they did it with a longbow in the cathedral close.)

ON THE CIRCUIT

The system of itinerant justices became so popular that Henry II (1158–89) reorganised the system, dividing England into circuits and setting up regular excursions from Westminster.

These judges were appointed from the King's Council. They were not trained in law and on their travels they had to take into account local customs and peculiarities. To help them do this juries were introduced, made up of local people who understood the customs of their neighbourhood, so justices could enforce these customs in the name of the king.

When they returned to Westminster the justices would compare notes, discuss their findings, sift through local customs and reject those that were unreasonable.

LET IT BE

So what happened to this system when new problems arose? The judges began to put into practice the principle of *stare decisis*, meaning let the decision stand.

Out of the different customs across the country a legal system was developed known as common law because it was in common to England and Wales.

AND THE REST IS HISTORY

Today in the UK there exist three major legal systems, each with its own legal rules, courts and legal professions.

ENGLAND AND WALES
Form one jurisdiction or legal area. Not since the early Middle Ages has Wales had its own legal system. The national courts for England and Wales: the High Court, Court of Appeal and the House of Lords are in London.

NORTHERN IRELAND
The legal system is similar in many ways to that of England and Wales, although it does have some unusual features. These are often connected to the political instability and violence that have been part of life in the province since it was formed. For example, there are no juries in terrorist trials in Northern Ireland.

SCOTLAND
Scotland had developed its own system of laws and courts before it joined with England and Wales. The Acts of Union in 1707 allowed these to continue and Scottish law remains different from English law today.

Today every independent country has its own legal systems based on common law, civil law or a mixture of both.

DARE TO BE DIFFERENT

Most English speaking countries have systems based on the common law system. However, nothing is simple.

The US system is based on common law, except for the state of Louisiana, which was colonised by the French and has a civil law system. Similarly Canada has a common law system, except in the French speaking province of Quebec, which bases its system on civil law.

EUROPEAN LAW

After the Second World War, countries in Western Europe began to work together in areas such as economics and defence. This led to the formation of the Council of Europe and of the North Atlantic Treaty Alliance (NATO) in 1949.

Putting aside years of mutual distrust, Germany with its manufacturing base and France with its agricultural strength began to see that they were stronger together than they were apart and in 1951 the Treaty of Paris expanded this co-operation to include Belgium, Luxembourg, the Netherlands and Italy.

Today, membership of the European Community (EC) has increased to include, among others, the UK, Greece, Denmark, Spain and Austria, and it is still growing.

Since 1972, when the UK signed the Treaty of Rome, the laws of the EC have in most cases been incorporated into UK law.

CHAPTER 3

A legal quiz
How much do you know?

Before reading further, it's time to find out how much you know about a legal career.

QUESTIONS

1. You need a legal degree if you want to follow a legal career in the UK.
   True or False?

2. Only barristers can speak in court.
   True or False?

3. Law is a white male dominated profession so it's difficult for a woman or anyone from an ethnic minority group to become a lawyer.
   True or False?

4. Any degree that has an element of law in it brings exemption from a part of legal training.
   True or False?

5. What is a training contract?

6. What do the letters CPS stand for?

7. What is a mini-pupillage?

8. There's no point in even thinking of a career as a barrister unless you have a degree from Oxford or Cambridge.
    True or False?

9. What do the letters LPC stand for?

10. What is tort?

ANSWERS

1. **False.** For details of the Institute of Legal Executives (ILEX route) see Chapter 5.

2. **False.** Solicitors have always been able to speak or have right of audience, as it is known, in magistrates' courts, county courts and in crown courts in the case of an appeal or a sentencing hearing committed from a magistrate's court.

    Since 1993, solicitors have been able to obtain full right of audience in the High Court, Crown Court, Court of Appeal and House of Lords after undergoing training and gaining an advocacy certificate. Relatively few solicitors have so far taken advantage of this opportunity.

    However, these increased advocacy rights are an important step in blurring the differences between barristers and solicitors and raise the question of whether one day the two professions will merge.

3. **False.** Times are definitely changing. Today there are
    more women graduates with first and upper second
    class law degrees than men.

    The number of women solicitors has more than doubled
    in the last ten years. In 2001, of the 7,595 students who
    enrolled with the Law Society, 62.3 per cent were
    women and 21.2 per cent were from ethnic minorities

    At the same time there were 2,761 practising female
    barristers in England compared with 7,573 males.

    There has been some negative publicity in recent years
    about the difficulties faced by members of ethnic
    minority groups. This included applicants who had been
    refused interviews by firms for training contracts when
    they applied under their own names, but were offered
    interviews when they adopted Anglicised names.

    However, each year the number of trainee solicitors
    from ethnic minority groups increases, making it easier
    for those who follow.

    Both the Law Society and the Bar Council are
    committed to equal opportunities and the Bar Council
    has its own equal opportunities officers.

4. **False.** Make sure when applying for degree courses that
    the courses are recognised by the Law Society and the
    Inns of Court. They need to include the Seven
    Foundations of Legal Knowledge required by the
    professional bodies (see Chapter 5).

    Not all legal degree courses are recognised and joint
    degree and combined degree courses, especially those
    where the law element is a minor component of a course,
    may not include a sufficiently substantial legal element.

    Graduates with a degree that is not recognised are
    faced with taking a further course before legal training,

which is time consuming and expensive. A list of recognised courses is available on the Law Society website (see useful addresses at the back of this book).

5. A training contract is the final stage of training for solicitors, when they are attached to qualified solicitors who advise and guide them and monitor their progress (see Chapter 7).

6. The letters CPS stand for the Crown Prosecution Service. Set up in 1985, the CPS is the national prosecution service and is responsible for almost all the criminal proceedings brought by the police in England and Wales.

7. Mini-pupillages are a great opportunity to see exactly what being a barrister entails. They last for around a week and many chambers offer them to young people at school and university (see Chapter 8).

8. **False.** Less than 20% of pupils coming to the Bar are from Oxford or Cambridge. The remainder come from a wide spread of universities. However, there is still a tendency for chambers to opt for graduates from the older, more traditional universities.

9. The letters LPC stand for the Legal Practice Course, the vocational one-year course taken by graduates intending to become solicitors before they move to a training contract (see Chapter 5).

10. Tort is one of the core subjects in the Seven Foundations of Legal Knowledge. It is classified as the law of obligation and covers issues such as negligence, defamation and intimidation (see Chapter 5).

What was you score? Were you surprised at how much or how little you knew?

Read on to find out about whether the law is right for you and, just as important – are you right for the law?

CHAPTER 4

Is a legal career right for you?

Are you right for a legal career?

You want a challenge?

Qualifying as a lawyer is certainly a challenge. There are obstacles to be overcome on the way and there is great satisfaction to be gained from achieving something that is difficult.

However, be careful that the buzz you get is not from the challenge rather than the job itself.

EMMA WILLIAMS IS A PRACTISING SOLICITOR

'From school onwards everybody kept telling me how hard it was to be a solicitor and not to be disappointed if I didn't make it.

This made me determined to prove them wrong. I worked really hard through university and through my postgraduate course and put great effort into gaining a training contract.

Two years on, I'm not at all sure that being a solicitor is what I want. It's hard to put my finger on it. The people I work with are great, the atmosphere in the office is quite relaxed. Still somehow I'm not sure the role I have at work is really me.

I fought so hard to achieve my goal, I possibly didn't give enough time to examining what the end result of my struggles would be.'

DECIDE FOR YOURSELF

Gaining a place on a legal degree course is an achievement in itself. Typical offers require A-level grades of AAB/ABB and Scottish Highers AAAAB/ABBBB.

This can lead to the assumption that academically bright pupils should take a law degree because they are capable of gaining a place, regardless of whether the course and the job to which it leads are right for the individual.

You might be capable of gaining a place on a degree course and of coming out with a good degree – but is that what you want?

Do you:

● see yourself as creative and artistic and enjoy working with your hands?

● pride yourself on being a free spirit, a real individual?

● find an office environment depressing and prefer to be in the open air?

● prefer a broad brush approach and find paying attention to the smallest detail boring?

● become stressed when people press you to complete work by a set time?

- like working on you own, find it difficult accommodating the needs of other people and avoid working as part of a team?

RIGHT OR WRONG?

There are no correct answers to the questions. They are merely the beginning of a period of self analysis you should put yourself through before making any decisions about a future career, legal or otherwise.

Remember that gaining the grades to study law is not sufficient reason for opting for a legal career.

What does make a good lawyer?

- A fascination for the law itself – how it developed, how it works, new legal developments

- A rational approach to the subject, pleasure in discovering the reasoning behind a legal decision

- Confidence to discuss matters verbally and to make points clearly

- Ability to get on well with people from different backgrounds

- Attention to detail

- Capacity to digest large amounts of information and pick out key points

- Good writing skills

- Ability to work long hours and deal with a heavy workload

- A team worker who finds working with other people satisfying and stimulating

- Self-motivation and strong personal organisational skills.

If you recognise yourself in this list of qualities then a law degree and possibly a legal career could be right for you.

But remember this book is a starting point. Do your homework. Find out as much as you can about different courses, training opportunities and aspects of legal work before taking action.

Wrong decisions can be expensive and demoralising.

CHAPTER 5

A career as a solicitor

WHAT EXACTLY DO SOLICITORS DO?

They are the people you visit when you want to make a will, buy a house or, looking on the darker side, when you have been charged with a criminal offence. Solicitors' clients are usually members of the public who need advice on legal matters.

There is a growing tendency for solicitors to specialise in a particular area of legal work, such as:

- Business and Commercial Law

- Property

- Probate

- Litigation (advising clients over disputes or disagreements). This includes:
  - Criminal law (crimes or public wrongs punishable by the state – such as murder, robbery or fraud)

- Civil law (disputes between individuals or businesses over issues such as personal injury or negligence)

- Environmental law – dealing with issues such as emissions and trading advice

- European law – the most active area is employment law.

Solicitors represent clients in magistrates' courts and county courts. More serious criminal cases are heard in the Crown Court where a solicitor will normally brief a barrister to speak for a client.

In the past 20 years becoming a solicitor has proved to be a highly popular career option and competition is tough.

WHERE DO THEY WORK?

PRIVATE PRACTICE
Eighty per cent of solicitors work in private practice. The size of these practices varies from two or three solicitors to huge legal firms employing vast numbers of lawyers.

Although the vast majority of solicitors work in private practice, there are good employment opportunities in other areas, as described below.

CROWN PROSECUTION SERVICE (CPS)
Since 1985 criminal prosecutions have been undertaken by the CPS, or Procurator Fiscal Service in Scotland, while the defence is carried out by lawyers in private practice.

The CPS prosecutes in court around 1.5 million cases every year. Not all criminal cases come to court. In order to do so cases must be considered to have a good chance of resulting in a conviction. Solicitors in the CPS advise the police on whether there is enough evidence to bring a prosecution case and when there is they carry out the pre-court preparation work.

GOVERNMENT
There are two main types of government work:

- Advising ministers and administrators on the law and the way in which it affects their departments

- Carrying out many of the tasks undertaken by solicitors in private practice for people who are under age or have a physical or mental ability that makes them unable to represent themselves.

Government legal work tends to be less well paid than private practice but it brings with it the chance to move from department to department and experience a variety of work, plus the chance to be involved in serious issues early in your career

LOCAL AUTHORITIES
Lawyers are employed by county councils, borough councils and district councils to give legal advice on issues affecting local government, such as childcare, licensing applications and planning.

INDUSTRY AND COMMERCE
Large organisations, including banks, insurance companies, manufacturing and commercial operations, have their own legal departments to look after their interests.

TRAINING TO BE A SOLICITOR

There are two stages of training:

- Academic – this is obtained by following either:
    - the law degree route
    - the non-law degree route
    - the ILEX route.

- Vocational
    - Stage I – completion of the Legal Practice course
    - Stage II – serving a two year training contract.

THE ACADEMIC STAGE

THE LAW DEGREE ROUTE

The most popular route is to take a law degree that is recognised as a qualifying law degree. by the Law Society. No particular A-level subjects are required for a place on a law course and science subjects are as acceptable as arts subjects. However, competition for places is strong. Typical offers from universities ask for A-level grades of AAB/ABB and for Scottish Highers AAAAB/ABBBB.

It is vital to make sure that the course you choose is recognised as covering the Foundations of Legal Knowledge is required by the Law Society and the General Council for the Bar.

THE FOUNDATIONS OF LEGAL KNOWLEDGE

These are:

● Obligations, including Contract, Restitution and Tort

● Criminal Law

● Equity and the Law of Trusts

● The Law of the European Union

● Property Law

● Public Law.

More detailed information about the Foundations of Legal Knowledge and a list of recognised courses is available on the Law Society website: www.lawsociety.org.uk.

Once you have obtained a recognised law degree, the next step is to complete the vocational stage, beginning with the Legal Practice Course.

ADVANTAGES OF THE LAW DEGREE ROUTE
This is the quickest way to qualify.
DISADVANTAGES
It means narrowing your study options at an early stage.

Stephen Brown is a solicitor specialising in licensing law.

When did you decide you wanted a law career?
I was fascinated by the law by the time I was at secondary school, so I had plenty of time to gain work experience. I studied for a law degree and then the LPC.

Did you have problems finding a training contract?
No, it wasn't difficult finding a contract. My problems started later. There was a recession at the time and none of the trainees in my year was offered a permanent post. I found a job with another legal firm but was made redundant within six months.

Did you stay in private practice?
I went into local government work, where my main areas of work were planning and environmental law, but I also dealt with public entertainment licences and taxi licences.

You're now back with a legal firm?
I work in the environmental, licensing and planning department of a legal firm. My clients are nightclub and restaurant owners, pub managers and tenants and breweries wanting liquor licences, or public entertainment licences.

Do you enjoy your job?
It's demanding and busy but I meet a lot of people and travel quite a lot, which makes it very interesting.

THE NON-LAW DEGREE ROUTE

THE COMMON PROFESSIONAL EXAMINATION (CPE) / POSTGRADUATE DIPLOMA IN LAW (PGDL)

Graduates with a first degree (BA or BSc) in any subject can take a course leading to the CPE/PGDL before going on to further legal training.

The CPE/PGDL conversion courses enable students to complete the academic stage of training by covering the foundation subjects over one year full-time or two years part-time or distance learning. The minimum entry qualification is usually a lower second class honours degree. There are 31 institutions in the country offering CPE/PGDL courses. A list of courses can be found on the Law Society website.

● Students on full-time courses are assessed in in each of the Foundations of Legal Knowledge and one other area of legal studies.

● Part-time and distance learning students must be assessed in four foundation subjects at the end of the first year and in the three remaining foundation subjects and the additional area of law at the end of the second year. Students must pass the first year assessments before moving on to the second year of the course.

After the successful completion of a CPE/PGDL course you can go on to a Legal Practice Course in the same way as a graduate with a law degree.

ADVANTAGES OF THE NON-LAW DEGREE ROUTE
You keep your study options open longer and you have the opportunity to study any academic subject to degree level.

DISADVANTAGES OF THE NON-LAW DEGREE ROUTE
You're studying for longer and face the cost of an additional year's study. Fees for a CPE/PGDL course are between £2,500 and £3,500. You also need to consider living expenses during this period although part-time study or distance learning can be combined with a job.

THE VOCATIONAL STAGE
Once the academic stage is completed, students move on to the vocational stage.

The first stage of vocational training is the Legal Practice Course (LPC), which is one year full-time and two years part-time and is run at institutions across the country.

LEGAL PRACTICE COURSE

This comprises a mixture of written examinations, accounts and skills assessments. Amongst other subjects, you will cover:

- **Compulsory Areas**

  - Business Law and Practice
  - Litigation (Civil and Criminal)
  - Property law and practice.

- **Pervasive Areas**

  - Professional conduct, client care and accounts
  - Financial services
  - Human rights.

- **Legal Skills**

  - Advocacy
  - Interviewing and advising
  - Legal writing and drafting
  - Practical legal research.

- **Elective Areas**

Students have to study three electives from a range of subjects. The choice of these is often based around the type of work to be undertaken during the training contract.

You need to apply for a place on an LPC course in the year before you want to start the course. Application forms are available from the LPC Central Applications Board (see Useful Addresses). In the case a of part-time course, you apply directly to the college. A list of recognised courses can be found on the Law Society website.

Scotland
After gaining a law degree, trainees take a postgraduate diploma in legal practice at a Scottish university followed by a two-year traineeship overseen by the Law Society of Scotland.

Northern Ireland
Solicitor training is known as apprenticeship and involves work in a solicitor's office under a master who is a qualified solicitor plus block release at the Institute of Professional Legal Studies. An apprenticeship lasts two years for postgraduate trainees and four years for trainees who do not have a degree.

THE TRAINING CONTRACT
The depressing news is that having reached this point in your career you face a high hurdle — finding a training contract.

This is where as a trainee you are attached to a firm of qualified solicitors, or another authorised training establishment, for the next two years or so. Their role is to advise and guide you while monitoring your progress.

The bad news is that no amount of academic qualifications will guarantee you a training contract. Figures suggest that almost 20% of applicants are disappointed. In order to be one of those who aren't, you need to do your research and market yourself as actively as possible.

See Chapter 7 for advice on gaining a training contract.

During your training contract period you need to complete the Professional Skills Course. This is divided into three compulsory courses:

● Finance and business skills

● Advocacy and communication skills

● Client care and professional standards.

On successful completion of a training contract you can pat yourself on the back and apply to the Law Society for admission as a solicitor.

THE ILEX ROUTE

You can become a solicitor without having a degree by following the Institute of Legal Executives (ILEX) or legal training route. Training is usually carried out on a part-time basis while working with a legal firm, although some colleges do run full-time courses.

QUALIFYING AS A LEGAL EXECUTIVE
The minimum educational requirements are:

● four GCSE passes at grades A–C in academic subjects including English

● two A-levels and one GCSE

● three AS-levels

- National Vocational Qualification (NVQ) Level 3

- the Institute of Legal Executives Preliminary Certificate in Legal Studies.

Mature students over the age of 25 years without formal qualifications can be considered on the basis of their business, commercial, academic or other experience.

To become a Member of the Institute of Legal Executives (M.Inst.L.Ex) you need to pass the membership examinations, which are set in two stages:

- **Level 3 Professional Diploma in Law (formerly known as Part 1 Examinations)** usually taken over two years. They are set at A-level standard and cover most of the areas of law and legal practice encountered in the legal profession.

  There are two routes:

  - Examination route consists of four papers covering the English legal system and essential elements of law and practice
  - Mixed assessment route includes a portfolio, case studies and one end of course examination.

  Study is usually part-time at a local college or by home study.

- **Level 4 Professional Diploma in Law (formerly known as Part 2 Examinations)** usually taken over two years, they are set at degree level and comprise one specialist practice paper and three associated law papers. Study is usually part-time at a local college or by home study.

The examinations are set twice a year and can all be taken at separate sittings. The majority of trainee legal executives complete the membership examinations over a four-year period taking two papers a year.

You don't need to have any legal employment experience to achieve membership status, but it is necessary to achieve fellowship status.

Fellowship of the Institute of Legal Executives (F.Inst.L.Ex)
In order to qualify as a fellow you need to:

- be over 25 years of age

- be a member of the Institute of Legal Executives

- have completed five years qualifying legal experience of which two years must have been completed after achieving M.Inst.L.Ex status.

QUALIFYING AS A SOLICITOR

THE ACADEMIC STAGE
As a legal executive wishing to qualify as a solicitor you need either to pass the Common Professional Examination or claim exemption by having passed corresponding papers in the M.Inst.L.Ex Part 2 examination.

THE VOCATIONAL STAGE
To complete this stage of training, legal executives must:

- be enrolled as a student member of the Law Society

- complete the Legal Practice course

- complete or be exempt from a two-year training contract

- complete the Professional Skills course.

The Legal Practice Course
Before starting this course, legal executives must either:

- be a M.Inst.L.Ex

- have served three years qualifying employment after the age of 18

- have been granted exemption from or completed the PGDL/CPE

- be a student member of the Law Society

- have been granted a certificate of completion of the academic stage.

OR

- be a F.Inst.L.Ex and meet the above requirements with the exception of the qualifying employment period.

THE ILEX ROUTE FOR LAW GRADUATES

Law graduates who have a qualifying law degree recognised by the Law Society, and who graduated within the last seven years may apply to be exempt from the academic part of the ILEX qualification. They take examinations in legal practice usually by studying part time while working full time in a solicitor's office or legal department.

These examinations can be completed in one or two years. Five years' qualifying employment under the supervision of a solicitor is required to qualify as a F.Inst.L.Ex. But remember that during this time you will be gaining experience and earning a salary.

THE GRADUATE ENTRY DIPLOMA

The Graduate Entry diploma (GED) is an alternative route for law graduates to gain the M.Inst.L.Ex qualification.

The diploma has been designed in conjunction with university law departments and can be taken alongside an existing law degree. It brings exemption from the academic and practice papers of the ILEX's professional qualification.

By gaining this diploma, law graduates complement their academic degree with membership of ILEX, thus enhancing their employment prospects. Details of institutions running the GED in conjunction with a qualifying law degree are available from ILEX (see Useful Addresses).

TRAINING CONTRACT

Fellows can claim exemption from the training contract provided they have completed the Legal Practice course and the Professional Skills course and have remained in continuous legal employment as a F.Inst.L.Ex before attending the course.

Members must complete the LPC and a two-year training contract and during this time complete the Professional Skills course.

ADVANTAGES OF THE ILEX ROUTE
You're in employment and you don't have to deal with the massive costs involved in degree and postgraduate courses.

DISADVANTAGES OF THE ILEX ROUTE
Achieving solicitor status by this route does take a long time.

Gillian Self is a fee earner with a firm of solicitors on the Isle of Wight.

What does your job involve?
I specialise in family law, which means I deal largely with divorce and matters arising from it, such as maintenance, pensions, contact with children and residence orders.

Recently, I've started undertaking some criminal work, which involves preparing cases for the criminal court.

What qualifications do you have?
I'm taking the ILEX route and have completed Part 1 of my studies and am on my way to gaining Part 2.

Do you intend to qualify as a solicitor?
My firm is very supportive and it's certainly something I'm thinking about seriously.

What form do your studies take?
For Part 1 I studied at evening class. My Part 2 studies are by distance learning. We're recommended to put aside the equivalent of half a day a week for study. This means a lot of evenings reading and rereading books.

Why did you choose ILEX?
Looking back to my school days, I think I was one of the many pupils categorised as being quiet and not academic. Nobody expected much of me and I certainly didn't expect a great deal of myself.

I left school at 16 and had a couple of clerical jobs before taking a job with a legal firm. As I started to be given more responsibility, I gained confidence and wanted to achieve more.

ILEX means I can study and earn a living at the same time, which is a realistic way for me to follow a legal career.

QUALIFICATION ROUTES ELSEWHERE

Scotland
The routes to qualification are through an approved law degree (LLB) course at a Scottish university or by undertaking a three-year pre-Diploma traineeship and sitting the Law Society examinations. Graduates with a degree in a subject other than law can take an accelerated law degree course and gain an ordinary degree in two years and an honours degree in three years.

Northern Ireland
Graduates with a degree in a subject other than law need to show the Law Society of Northern Ireland that they have a satisfactory level of legal knowledge. The way to do this is by taking the

Bachelor of Legal Science degree at Queen's University Belfast. This is a conversion course lasting two years full time and from three to five years part time.

Anyone over the age of 29 who has been employed in a solicitor's practice for seven years and can satisfy the Law Society of Northern Ireland that he or she has gained the necessary knowledge and experience can begin training as a solicitor.

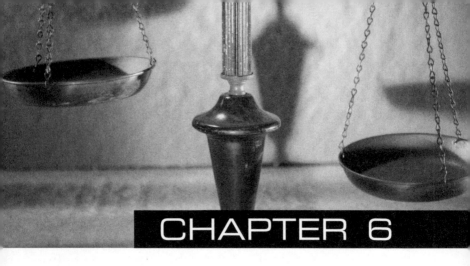

CHAPTER 6

A career as a barrister

WHAT DO BARRISTERS DO?

Barristers are often called counsel. There are around 9,000 of them in England and Wales. They are advocates and specialist legal advisers, trained to provide independent legal advice to clients on the strengths and weaknesses of their legal case. Their main work is to conduct cases in court. When a case comes to trial in a superior or a criminal court it is usually barristers who present the case and cross-examine witnesses.

Under what is known as the 'Cab Rank Rule', if a barrister is available to act on someone's behalf he or she must take the case.

WHERE DO THEY WORK?

Barristers may be self-employed or employed. If they are self-employed, they must practise as a sole practitioner. Barristers who are self-employed usually practise from offices, known as chambers, which they share with other barristers. This enables them to share the cost of rent and administrative services.

Barristers with three years' experience can practise independently. This means they can work from home if they choose.

Barristers are also employed by organisations including government departments, which use their legal skills in ways similar to those in which they employ solicitors.

Government barristers also prosecute on behalf of their department, for example tax fraud or drug smuggling.

There are openings for barristers with the Crown Prosecution Service (CPS).

TRAINING TO BE A BARRISTER/ADVOCATE

There are four main stages that you must complete in order to become a barrister:

- Academic stage

- Vocational stage

- Pupillage

- Continuing Professional Development.

ACADEMIC STAGE

Entrants need a law degree, or a non-law degree plus a CPE/PGDL conversion course. Persons who do not have a degree but have a professional qualification may be eligible to apply through the mature students entry route.

While there are no specific subjects that should be studied prior to university at either GCSE or A-level, some chambers and employers do consider the grades gained in these examinations when making their selections for pupillages.

The standard requirement for completion of the academic stage is a lower second class honours degree.

When considering law degree courses you need to make sure that the course you choose is a qualifying law degree that will lead on directly to the vocational stage of training (see Chapter 5). A list of qualifying degrees can be found in the training section of the Bar Council website (see Useful Addresses).

VOCATIONAL STAGE

BAR VOCATIONAL COURSE (BVC)

The BVC aims to make sure students intending to become barristers gain the skills and knowledge they need to cope with the specialised training they receive in their pupillage.

It's not easy to gain a place on a BVC. In 2002/2003, 2,067 applications were made for 1,406 full-time places, which means 32% of applicants did not gain a place.

The BVC runs for one year full time and two years part time. It is available at eight colleges. They are:

BPP Law School, London
The College of Law, London
Inns of Court School of Law, City University, London
The University of Northumbria, Newcastle
Cardiff Law School
University of the West of England, Bristol
Manchester Metropolitan University
Nottingham Law School.

Part-time courses are available at the Inns of Court School of Law and the BPP Law School.

Since 2002 you can apply online for a BVC place on www.bvconline.co.uk. Course fees range from around £7,000 to £10,000, with courses in London being the most expensive.

The main skills taught on the BVC are:

- Case work skills
    Case preparation
    Legal research

- Written skills
    General written skills
    Opinion writing (giving written advice)
    Drafting (drawing up various types of documents)

- Interpersonal skills
    Conference skills (interviewing clients)
    Negotiation
    Advocacy (court or tribunal appearances)

- The main areas of knowledge taught are:
    Criminal litigation and remedies
    Criminal litigation and sentencing
    Evidence
    Professional ethics
    Two optional subjects selected from a choice of six.

Assessment of skills and knowledge is done in a number of ways, including multiple-choice tests, written papers and practical exercises.

INNS OF COURT
Before registering for your BVC vocational training, you must become a member of one of the Inns of Court. Many students choose to do this at an early date in order to use an inn's facilities. Your choice of inn has no effect on the area of law you want to practise or your choice of pupillage or tenancy. There are four Inns of Court, all based in London:

    Lincoln's Inn
    Inner Temple
    Middle Temple
    Gray's Inn.

In order to be called to the bar, you need to complete 12 qualifying units. These can be achieved in a number of different ways:

- weekends either in the inn or at a residential centre

- education days (these are primarily for out of London students)

- education dinners (with lectures or talks)

- domus dinners (when students and seniors dine together)

- social dinners.

The weekend events count as three units, the days as two and the dinners as one unit.

The inns also organise advocacy events for students and have their own student societies, which hold debating and social events.

PUPILLAGE

This is the final stage in becoming a barrister and it is a very tough one. In the year 2000/2001, 766 pupillage vacancies were filled.

Not all students will obtain a pupillage at the first attempt. (See Chapter 8 for advice on improving your chances of gaining a pupillage.)

Pupillage is an opportunity to learn on the job while being supervised by an experienced barrister, called a pupil supervisor. It takes place either in barristers' chambers or in a pupillage training organisation and is in two parts:

- months 1–6, known as the non-practising six

- months 7–12, known as the practising six.

During the non-practising six you accompany your supervisor to court, read their pleadings and other documents. You continue with this in the practising six while taking on your own cases with the permission of your supervisor.

During your pupillage, in order to be entitled to a full qualification certificate, you are required by the Bar Council to attend:

- an advocacy training course

- an advice to counsel course

- a forensic accountancy course.

Advocacy training should be completed in the first six months of a pupillage.

The advice to counsel course aims to provide a bridge between pupillage and practice and covers:

- personal and business finance

- European Convention on Human Rights

- conditional fees

- ethics, professional conduct and complaints procedure

- professional relationships with solicitors

- practical advice from the bench about first appearances in court.

The forensic accountancy course introduces practitioners to the use of financial and accounting information in practice at the Bar.

Further information about pupillages is available on the Bar Council website: www.legaleducation.org.uk.

FINDING AND APPLYING FOR A PUPILLAGE

All pupillage providers are required to advertise their vacancies on the website (www.pupillageonline.org.uk). There are two application systems:

- OLPAS – online application system

- Non-OLPAS system – traditional paper based application system.

Around 150 pupillage providers are on the OLPAS system. Candidates can choose to apply to 12 of them and all these applications are made online. The first part of the application is common to all providers and is filled in only once. The second part is specific to the individual provider and is filled in separately for each application.

Once the application is released into the OLPAS system it is sent directly to the pupillage provider. The provider and the candidate then communicate by email through the OLPAS system.

Not all providers are on the OLPAS system and candidates can apply to as few or as many of these as they wish.

COSTS

The good news is that as a pupil you are paid at least £833.33 a month plus reasonable training expenses. Many pupillage providers also guarantee earnings in the practising six months.

AND ELSEWHERE –

TRAINING FOR ADVOCATES IN SCOTLAND

Trainee advocates are called intrants and they take the full-time Diploma in Legal Practice course as trainee solicitors. Following this they train for 21 months in a solicitor's office for which they receive a salary. The final stage of training is nine months of pupillage known as 'devilling', spent with a member of the Scottish Bar. During this time they must pass the Faculty of Advocates' exams for which there are no formal lecture courses.

TRAINING FOR BARRISTERS IN NORTHERN IRELAND

Students wishing to become barristers in Northern Ireland must take the competitive exam for a place on the vocational course run by the Institute of Professional Legal Studies. There are only 25 places a year and around 350 applicants. This is followed by six months' pupillage under a barrister before a pupil receives a Practising Certificate and becomes a barrister.

Training Contracts –
How to find one

'Be aware of the need to market yourself, to create opportunities to get a job and use every opportunity carefully to your advantage.'
(from *Qualifying as a Solicitor*, published by the Law Society)

It's easy to become depressed at the hurdles to be overcome in a legal career.

You work hard at your A-levels because you know that without good grades you won't be offered a place on a law degree course. You gain a degree and complete your Legal Practice Course only to discover that competition for training contracts is intense and without one you cannot qualify as a solicitor.

ALWAYS LOOK ON THE BRIGHT SIDE

Be as positive as possible and don't fall into the trap of thinking everything is a foregone conclusion and you don't stand a chance.

Firms can afford to be fussy. Some top names calculate that they have 1,000 applicants for 100 training contracts. Not only do they expect an upper second class or first class honours degree, they also want 24 UCAS points and at least a B grade in GCSE maths and English language.

The same firms are also more likely to target legal departments in the older, more traditional universities, which demand the highest entry requirements, rather than the newer universities. However, as a spokesman from a legal firm pointed out: 'That doesn't mean we're not interested in individual students from all universities'.

They are looking for people who will stay with them long term. While it is usual for graduates going into other areas of work to look for new jobs after three or four years, this is not the case in the legal profession. It is not unusual for individuals to join a firm as trainees and remain there throughout their career, eventually becoming partners.

As a trainee you will receive a salary during the period of your training contract of up to £28,000 a year in the larger firms in London and £18,500 in other areas.

However, it costs a firm around £125,000 to train you and so it is in their interests to find the right people for their training and many of them put a great deal of time and energy into this procedure.

THINK POSITIVE

It's easy to become disheartened and take the view that looking for a training contract is hardly worth the effort.

It's in your own interests to fight negative thinking. Throughout your life you may find reasons to convince yourself something is not worth doing, because you're bound to fail anyway – and that is the biggest recipe of all for failure.

You might not have been to public school, you might have a regional accent and you might have curly hair. Instead of thinking up reasons why you *won't* succeed, put your energies into your campaign for *success*.

BE KIND TO YOURSELF

What is needed is calm, careful planning, not desperation. Try to keep a sense of proportion even if things are not going the way you want.

Aim for balance in your life. Don't spend all your time with friends who are either in the same situation as yourself, talking endlessly about how miserable you all are, or, on the other hand, with those who have training contracts and who make you feel like a failure in comparison.

Don't lock yourself away. Keep in contact with friends and family, including those who have no connection with the law. Eat properly, take some exercise and don't drift into that dangerously hamster-like existence where you stay up most of the night and sleep the daylight hours away.

TO BE FOREWARNED IS TO BE FOREARMED

At the beginning of this book you were advised to plan ahead and to think carefully about exactly what sort of legal career you wanted before applying for undergraduate courses.

Decisions need to be made well in advance in the world of legal training. Undergraduates taking a law degree should be applying for training contracts at the end of their second year, while those studying for a non-legal degree should be doing so by the end of their final undergraduate year.

The type of questions you need to sort out at an early date include:

● What do you really want from your career?

● What sort of working environment do you want?

- In which sector of the law would you like to specialise?

- In which area do you want to live and work?

Don't skip past these questions because you're prepared to go anywhere and do anything. That way you're not being realistic – you're merely avoiding important issues.

Is your heart set on working for a large multinational organisation in a city, or would you prefer a smaller firm where you know everybody and everyone knows you?

While you can't afford to be too exclusive, you need to consider carefully where you want to live for what may be the rest of your working life. Is it important to stay within reasonable travelling distance of your family? If it is, perhaps you should limit your search for a training contract to a particular region of the country. Are you, on the other hand, addicted to urban buzz? If so then you could look at firms in four or five major cities.

Once you've decided on your geographical area the next step is to research firms in that area and consider carefully those that seem to offer what you're looking for.

WORK PLACEMENTS

These play a vital role in gaining a training contract. Around 25% of trainees are offered training contracts by firms where they had work placements. For further information, see Chapter 9.

DETECTIVE WORK

The Law Society recommends the following methods for finding out about legal firms with a view to applying for a training contract:

- Visit law fairs at your university or college and talk to as many people as possible

- Get on to firms' websites and find out what they have to say about themselves

- The following websites are gold mines of information:
  - Prospects legal website – www.prospects.csu.ac.uk
  - The *Legal Times* website – www.legalease.co.uk
  - The *Law Society Gazette* – www.lawsociety.org.uk
  - The Law Society training website – www.training.lawsociety.org.uk

- So are the directories listed below:
  - *The Legal 500* by John Pritchard, published by Legalease
  - *Chambers & Partners Directory*, published by Chambers & Partners Publishing
  - *Solicitors and Barristers*, published by the National Law Directory Society
  - *Solicitors' Regional Directories*, published by The Law Society

- Also useful are:
  - *The Lawyer* magazine
  - *The Legal Action Bulletin* – available from:
  - The Legal Action Group,
  - 242 Pentonville Road,
  - London
  - N9 UW

LIFE DOESN'T END WITH THE BIG FIRMS

There are currently nearly 10,000 law firms in private practice, of which only 449 have 11 or more partners, 1,100 have between five and ten partners, 3,800 have between two and four partners and 4,400 are sole practitioners. These figures show very clearly that confining training contract applications to large firms is not a good idea.

Other possible providers of a training contract are:

- the Crown Prosecution Service (see Useful Addresses)

- the Government Legal Service (see Useful Addresses)

- industry and commerce

- the Public Sector.

HOW MUCH IS ENOUGH?

It is common sense to find out as much as possible about a firm before applying for a training contract, but how much should you know?

Firms are looking for a sense of commercial awareness because, after all, they exist to make a profit, so an understanding of the world of business gleaned from the business sections of broadsheet national newspapers and legal magazines is expected.

You also need to demonstrate that you genuinely want to work in a particular firm through an awareness of the type of client it attracts and its recent activities, which can be found on a firm's website.

QUALITY NOT QUANTITY

Your application form needs to reflect the knowledge you have. Firms are looking for someone who will fit in with the ethos of their organisation, who really wants to work for them and who will bring in a return for their investment.

Firms are not impressed by an application form that shows no specific knowledge and that has clearly been sent off with 50 or so others in the mistaken belief that by trawling the net as widely as possible you're bound to catch something.

Make sure you spend sufficient time on each application and show those who will be reading it that not only are you right for them, but that you believe they are right for you. On a practical note, keep a photocopy of every application form you send off, then if you are called for an interview you can check what you wrote beforehand.

THE ASSESSMENT DAY

The next hurdle could well be the assessment day. A growing number of legal firms are opting for this method of selection, so be prepared.

Together with a group of other potential trainees you'll spend a day with a firm taking part in different activities. No two firms' assessment days are the same, but be ready for:

- Communication and role play exercises where, for example, you may be asked to interview a new client

- A formal interview with a partner based on your application form

- Psychometric testing. (These are usually short multiple-choice, written tests. Their aim is not to test what you know, but to give an indication of the type of person you are)

- Lunch with the assessment group and members of the firm.

Firms are not interested in the level of your legal knowledge on assessment days. They want to learn about you as a person. The possibility for advance preparation may be limited, but bear in mind that your formal interview will be based on what you wrote on your application form, so a spot of revision is essential.

HONESTY IS THE BEST POLICY

Don't pretend to be someone you're not in order to try and impress people. You could be working for a firm for the rest of your working life and that's a long time to keep up a pretence. Be yourself, but the best of yourself.

Present yourself well. Wear clothes that are neat and profess- ional, but also comfortable. Shoes that cripple you, a shirt that strangles you, or a hairstyle that refuses to stay in place are not going to help you on the day.

Show a genuine interest in the people you meet and try not to see everyone else as competition. Lunch is usually a good chance to ask informal questions and to find out what a firm is really like. Relax and enjoy it, but steer clear of alcohol if it's on offer and keep a clear head for the afternoon.

Don't feel you have to ask questions in order to stand out from the rest. There may be points you want to raise but then again there may not, and asking something just for the sake of letting your voice be heard can be counter-productive.

PRACTICE MAKES PERFECT

University careers services often run assessment day workshops. These are well worth attending and an excellent way of preparing yourself for what could lie ahead.

CHAPTER 8

Pupillages —
How to find one

A pupillage is the final part of barrister training. The structure of pupillages is covered in Chapter 6.

While you will be qualified as a barrister on completion of your Bar Vocational Course (BVC), in order to practise you must complete 12 months' pupillage.

AN EARLY START

To give yourself the best possible opportunities in such a competitive environment you need to start early. Chambers look to recruit pupils a year to two years into the future.

There is a set timetable for applications. This specifies that:

● no pupillage offers can be made before July of the penultimate year of a legal degree course and the final year of a non-legal degree course

- no pupillage offers can be made between the examination period, which is May to the end of July

- pupillage offers remain open for 14 days.

MINI-PUPILLAGES

These are vitally important opportunities to see for yourself the truth about life in chambers and how one chamber differs from another. Typically, they last around a week. They can begin when you're still at school and carry on throughout university. Many barristers do five or six mini-pupillages in order to gain a rounded view of the role of a barrister.

Mini-pupillages also provide a vital opportunity to make an impression on chambers and to demonstrate your potential. Chambers will be looking for legal experience as well as academic qualifications from pupils and mini-pupillages are an important way of gaining such experience.

ONE STEP AT A TIME

By the time you apply for a pupillage you should have a strong idea of the area of law in which you wish to practise. The pattern of your future working life will be dependent on these decisions. For instance, if you opt for commercial law work you will spend a great deal of time in your chambers doing written work. Whereas if you choose criminal work you will be in court almost every day.

Before applying for a pupillage with a chamber you need to carry out your own research into:

- the type of work undertaken by a particular chamber and the type of reputation they have for this work

- how well organised a pupillage is at a particular chamber

- the levels of work available for junior tenants. This is because your chances of being offered a tenancy at the end of your pupillage are dependent on this

- whether you would fit in with other members of a chamber and enjoy being there for the rest of your working life.

ASKING QUESTIONS

So where do you find such information? Dining with other students and members of the legal profession helps you to feel comfortable socialising in a legal environment and provides a valuable opportunity for gaining some inside information.

Advocacy courses run by all the Inns of Court provide excellent training plus a chance to mix with legal professionals and to find out about the current state of play.

There are student officers at all the Inns of Court who can provide up to date and realistic advice about pupillage opportunities.

Once again mini-pupillages are the ideal way to carry out your own on-the-spot research.

SELLING YOURSELF

The advice on gaining a training contract in Chapter 7 is also relevant to finding a pupillage.

Unless you find yourself unable to contemplate leaving London, applying for pupillages outside the capital can be a good idea.

Chambers are looking for confident, articulate, well-rounded team players, not just legal beagles, so don't neglect other aspects of your life.

A TENANCY

Becoming a tenant in a chamber means after years of training and effort you are on the first rung of your career as a barrister.

Around nine months into a pupillage the decision is taken whether or not to offer a pupil a tenancy. It is by no means a certainty that a pupil will be offered a tenancy, and many are not.

If it doesn't happen, you can either apply for a third session of pupillage with another chamber or apply for a tenancy somewhere else.

CHAPTER 9

Vacation placements and mini-pupillages

SUMMER FUN

You've worked hard and the summer beckons. What will it bring: a spell in the local supermarket followed by inter-railing across Europe, a trip to Thailand with a couple of mates who know of all the best beach parties, or a chance to rest the brain and develop the tan while Greek island hopping?

Sadly, if you're really serious about a legal career your priority for the summer is more likely to be focused on Manchester rather than Majorca and Liverpool rather than Limnos.

The summer vacation brings with it a chance to gain the practical experience that will support your legal studies and lift you a step above others when applying for training contracts and pupillages.

HOW LONG DO THEY LAST?

Mini-pupillages usually last around a week, while vacation placements may be longer – up to around three weeks.

The aim is to give students a view of what life is like doing a particular job within an organisation. Your time could be spent doing a variety of things. On a mini-pupillage you might spend most of your time with a single barrister or you might have a chance to visit different areas of chambers.

On a vacation placement with a legal firm you could undertake a range of opportunities, such as shadowing different individuals, visiting departments, going to court, attending meetings and talking to members of staff.

Some organisations run a 'buddy' scheme where students on placements are paired with young members of staff who look after them and chat to them informally.

WHAT'S IN FOR ME?

The answer is a very great deal, especially if you play your cards right. Vacation placements are a chance to learn a lot and nothing is as valuable as first-hand experience.

HOW CAN I MAKE A GOOD IMPRESSION?

This is perhaps the wrong approach. Rather than wondering what people are thinking of you, concentrate on what you can gain from them:

- Be observant, notice what is going on, how people handle different situations, how they allocate their time

- Be enthusiastic about your placement and don't keep telling people how your friends are all lying on a Spanish beach and you wish you were there, even if the rain hasn't stopped for days

- Ask questions, but make sure you do so at the right time. You have an enquiring mind and there's a lot to learn, but don't leap on people like an overenthusiastic puppy the moment they've put the phone down after a 30-minute conversation with a client

- Be professional and discreet. Don't be tempted to enter into 'office politics' or to repeat comments or information you hear

- Be punctual and dress in a way that is comfortable and appropriate

- Be willing to do whatever you're asked, even if popping out to buy two ham rolls and a packet of crisps doesn't quite fit in with your legal ambitions.

HOW DO I FIND A VACATION PLACEMENT?

In some cases finding a vacation placement is as difficult, if not more so, than finding a training contact, so you'll need to put some time and effort into the procedure.

As a first step, look at yourself. What are your ultimate ambitions? Think about your strengths, the skills and experiences that are going to help you to achieve those aims. What are your weaknesses and how can you overcome them? Where do you lack experience and how can you gain it?

Then start considering the firms and organisations that are likely to offer what you're looking for. A good first point of contact is law fairs, where you can visit stands, have a chat and find out what is on offer.

APPLYING YOURSELF

Application for a vacation placement is often by completing a written form. Make sure you give yourself enough time to fill it in properly. Don't put this off until the last possible moment and do it in a rush.

Find out as much as you can about the firm concerned and show in your application that you have a sound knowledge of its activities. Advice on doing this is given in Chapter 7.

Don't forget the basics. In the words of one legal practitioner: 'Passages of information lifted directly from a firm's own promotional material is not going to impress anyone.'. Spelling the name of a firm or an individual incorrectly on an envelope or application form is not going to win you any brownie points either.

Large firms may run assessment days at which they select students for vacation placements. Advice on dealing with these is given in Chapter 7.

IF AT FIRST YOU DON'T SUCCEED

The summer vacation is approaching fast and you haven't got a placement. What do you do? Your friends will soon be off to the sun, do you give up and join them?

There are still plenty of opportunities to gain that much needed practical experience during the vacation.

You've not had any success with your applications to large firms running vacation placements. Then another possibility is to turn your attention to smaller firms, to be found on almost every high street.

Other possibilities are voluntary organisations, government agencies, local councils and Citizens' Advice Bureaux and in-house legal departments of commercial and industrial organisations.

When you're tempted to give up, just remind yourself of the importance of practical experience to your future career and steel yourself to write another letter or to make one more phone call.

CHAPTER 10

Making a difference —
Giving added value to your applications

You're well aware of the difficulties in gaining a pupillage or a training contract and a job afterwards.

You've taken on board the advice about long-term planning and on making the best of yourself on application forms, assessment days and interviews. Is there anything else you can do to show how serious you are in pursuing a legal career, whatever the difficulties?

COMBINING THEORY AND PRACTICE

The work of both solicitors and barristers demands a combination of theoretical and practical skills. In both cases a high level of academic knowledge is required, but at the same time you need to:

- think quickly

- express yourself clearly and put over complicated matters in a way that can be understood by people who have no legal training

- get on well with people from different backgrounds

- be self-motivated with good organisational skills

- enjoy working as part of a team.

Proving you possess these skills is more difficult than demonstrating academic ability, yet these are just as necessary for success in a legal career.

WHAT ELSE CAN I DO?

There are a growing number of ways in which you can gain valuable practical skills, make useful contacts and have the satisfaction of knowing that you are doing some good.

PRO BONO WORK

Pro bono work is the provision of free or subsidised legal advice for people who would not otherwise have access to it.

Today, legal aid or public funding is only available to a very small group of people. Even those who earn the minimum wage are unlikely to be eligible. This leaves a great number of people for whom legal advice at £100 an hour is completely out of reach. Pro bono work aims to do something towards bridging this gap.

US origins
Pro bono work began in the US where there has never been a publicly funded legal system and where there has long been a tradition of lawyers and law school students undertaking such work.

In contrast, the legal aid system established in the UK in 1948 did until relatively recently provide legal aid for the majority of people who couldn't afford private fees.

SOLICITORS PRO BONO GROUP (SPBG)

This was established in 1996 by Lord Phillips of Sudbury and a group of solicitors who realised that solicitors across the country were undertaking pro bono work and, in order to benefit the people most in need, a co-ordinated approach was needed.

Today, the SPBG is a charity with a complete mix of members, including students, solicitors, voluntary bodies, organisations and corporations. Members don't undertake to carry out a set amount of pro bono work. However, they are required to ensure that any work they undertake is of a high standard.

The SPBG is concerned that pro bono work is never seen as a second rate service. Student members are properly supervised and insured.

Core costs and the running of the group are almost entirely funded by membership fees. Students pay £15 a year for information and support on pro bono projects.

STUDENT GROUP

The SPBG has been involved in setting up practical clinics at universities and law schools where students have an opportunity to give legal advice. The group aims to establish its network across the UK from London to other major cities and into rural areas.

THE BAR PRO BONO UNIT

Also set up in 1996, the Bar Pro Bono Unit now has 1,200 barrister members. Each member promises to give three days unpaid work a year, which means 30,000 hours of free legal work are available each year.

One of the unit's aims is to ensure that the barrister undertaking a pro bono case is as experienced as a paid barrister undertaking similar work.

The Bar Pro Bono Unit works closely with the SPBG and a large number of referrals to the unit come from the SPBG.

In order to work as a barrister with the Bar Pro Bono Unit you need to have reached the second six of your pupillage. However, there are opportunities to work on other projects.

BAR IN THE COMMUNITY
This is open to BVC students as well as pupils and barristers. The aim of Bar in the Community is to link members to charitable organisations that would benefit from having somebody with legal expertise on their management committees.

FREE REPRESENTATION UNIT
Volunteer advocates are made up of BVC and LPC students. They undertake work for the Free Representation Unit for clients with limited means who are not eligible for legal aid. They appear before Employment Appeals Tribunals, Social Security Commissioners and the Criminal Injuries Compensation Appeal Panel.

Volunteers have access to the Free Representation Unit library and office facilities and are supported by two specialist caseworkers.

IN-HOUSE ADVICE CENTRES
A number of law schools run what are effectively becoming in-house legal advice centres. These offer students an opportunity to give advice to clients on legal matters. Their work is closely supervised by a barrister or a lawyer and the cases are carefully selected for their suitability for student involvement. Student work is limited to advising clients.

STREET LAW
This began at Georgetown University, Washington DC and is now established in over 50 US law schools, with programmes in India, South Africa, Eastern Europe and Mongolia. The first UK Street Law scheme was piloted in 1993 at the University of Derby.

Today, most law schools in the UK run Street Law projects of various kinds. These take the form of teams of students going out into the community to talk to groups about the law as it relates to them. Groups can be based in schools, colleges and prisons. They can be made up of asylum seekers, tenants, young people or school pupils. The sessions for young people fit into the study of citizenship, which became a National Curriculum subject in 2002.

A Street Law team finds out from a group the issues that concern it. Having identified these they go away and carry out their research, returning to give a presentation to the group and answer questions, which may involve further research. This way the group receives an overview of a particular area of law and individuals in the team have a chance to develop research and presentation skills.

A typical example of such work could be a group of residents eager to make improvements to the area in which they live. The Street Law team would undertake research into housing law and explain to the group how these laws affect them and their proposed activities.

Members of any group who need to take matters further are referred to other sources of help. All the work undertaken by the students is overseen by qualified barristers and solicitors.

THE BENEFITS OF PRO BONO WORK
It is estimated that over 50% of law students are involved in pro bono work of one type or another.

You can't undertake such work if you are motivated only by ideas of self-advancement. You need enthusiasm for the projects in which you are involved. You have to be prepared to give up valuable time for the work and to do this well you need to have a genuine desire to make a difference.

Having said that, pro bono work brings with it a chance to hone your skills and to make contact with people who could well affect your career in a positive way.

FURTHER INFORMATION
The Students' Initiative of the Solicitors Pro Bono Group keeps a database of people interested in volunteering and the opportunities available. Visit its website:
www.students.probonogroup.org.uk/volunteering

Other websites with information on pro bono work include:

● The Bar Pro Bono Unit – www.barprobono.org.uk

● The Solicitors Pro Bono Group – www.probonogroup.org.uk

● The College of Law – www.college-of-law.co.uk

The websites of UK law schools should have this information, too.

MOOTING

WHAT IS IT?
Mooting is the oral presentation of a legal issue or problem and is possibly the nearest a student can get to appearing in court while still at university. In some law schools mooting is compulsory, while at others it is completely voluntary. In either case mooting is a useful supplement to a law degree and can also be enjoyed by non-lawyers as the amount of legal knowledge required is not enormous.

HOW DOES IT WORK?
In a moot two pairs of advocates argue a fictitious legal appeal case in front of a judge, who is usually a lecturer or postgraduate student. To win you don't necessarily have to win the legal case, but you have to make the best presentation of your legal arguments.

Moots are held internally by law schools and universities. There are also a number of moots held nationally every year.

PREPARATION
Mooters have to prepare their arguments thoroughly in advance. During the moot itself the aim is to provide a courtroom atmosphere, with mooters maintaining a suitable courtroom manner and addressing each other as they would in court.

WHAT WILL I GAIN FROM MOOTING?
It is a useful way of developing the legal skills of analysis and interpretation and the personal skills of argument and public speaking. Mooting can be hard work but it's also great fun.

Both pro bono work and mooting are important ways of showing how seriously you take your career aims and as such are well regarded by chambers and legal firms.

'Anyone applying for pupillage . . . should be a first rate lawyer . . . Working with FRU (Free Representation Unit) or other voluntary work of a similar nature and mooting or public speaking would also be helpful.' (Broadway House Chambers)

HOW CAN I FIND OUT MORE?

Student law societies usually run their own mooting programme. Details of national and international mooting competitions can be found on www.mootingnet.org.uk

CHAPTER 11

Can I afford the cost of training to become a lawyer?

The cost of becoming a barrister or a solicitor is heavy and financial difficulties account for a great many students changing their plans and opting for a career unrelated to law.

Both the Law Society and the Bar Council recognise financial difficulties over funding as a major concern to law students, especially those who do not receive financial support from their parents.

THE COST OF UNDERGRADUATE STUDIES

The National Union of Students calculates that the average student leaves university after three years with a first degree and debts of around £15,000.

THE COST OF POSTGRADUATE STUDIES

The fees for either a Bar Vocational Course (BVC) or a Legal Practice Course (LPC) are between £7,000 and £10,000. Then there are living expenses during the course, which, based on the NUS calculations bring the total cost for the year to around £17,000, leaving you with debts in the region of £32,000.

If you take a non-law degree and opt for a conversion course before going on to BVC or LPC studies, your debts will be nearer £45,000.

ADDITIONAL SUPPORT FOR UNDERGRADUATE STUDIES

GENERAL ACCESS FUNDS AND HARDSHIP FUNDS

These are distributed by colleges and can take the form of cash payments or repayable loans. To be eligible you have to show that you have applied for all other sources of funding, including a student loan. The minimum payment is £100 and the maximum is £3,500 a year.

Colleges set their own criteria for distributing loans and success often depends on how much of their fund allocation remains at the time of your application. The best way forward is to seek advice from your college students' union or counselling service.

OPPORTUNITY BURSARIES

Since 2001 bursaries of up to £2,000 for a three-year course have been available from certain institutions for full-time under-graduate degree courses. To qualify you need to:

● be under 21 years old at the start of the course

● have attended a school or college within an Excellence in Cities or an Education Action Zone or have received an Education Maintenance Allowance (if funds allow, colleges can offer bursaries to students who don't meet these criteria as long as they meet the others)

- have had little or no experience of higher education (this also applies to your family), have a family income of less than £20,000 or be receiving means-tested benefits.

FINANCIAL SUPPORT FOR POSTGRADUATE LEGAL STUDY

As a postgraduate student you are not eligible for a government student loan.

DISCRETIONARY AWARDS

You may be eligible for a discretionary award from your local authority. Criteria for these awards are set by each authority and vary considerably from area to area. Where they are available they are very limited. If you are interested in applying, contact your authority for dates and put your application in as early as possible.

LOAN SCHEMES – HIGH STREET BANKS

Loans at favourable rates are available from high street banks. These include:

- HSBC – postgraduate studies loan

- Barclays Bank – professional studies loan

- Royal Bank of Scotland – the law student loan scheme. (See Useful Addresses.)

CAREER DEVELOPMENT LOANS

These are operated on behalf of the Department for Education and Skills by four banks:

- Barclays Bank

- Clydesdale Bank

- Co-operative Bank

- Royal Bank of Scotland.

They are available to pay for 80% of the course fees on vocational courses and may include payments for living expenses where courses are full-time. The minimum age for a loan is 21 years old and the maximum is 65 years.

To be considered for a loan you have to provide evidence that you intend to use the resulting qualification to gain employment in the UK or the European Community and show that you are unable to fund the course from other sources.

The minimum loan is £300 and the maximum £8,000. Interest on the loan is paid by the government during the course and for three months afterwards. This is extended to 12 months when you go into practical training such as a training contract or pupillage.

Information on Career Development Loans is available from participating banks and from branches of Jobcentre Plus.

LAW SOCIETY BURSARY SCHEME
The scheme consists of a variety of grants and loans. The fund is very limited and there are competitive elements and hardship criteria. To be eligible you need to be outstanding in achievement or dedication and genuinely in need of support with no other access to major funding.

Further information and an application form can be obtained from Information Services, tel: 01527 504455 (24 hours).

BAR COUNCIL SCHOLARSHIP TRUST
This provides assistance during pupillage in the form of interest-free loans up to £5,000 depending on your individual circumstances.

INNS OF COURT SCHOLARSHIPS
In the year 2000/01, the Inns of Court provided 327 BVC awards: 114 were for amounts between £5,000 and £9,999 and 70 were above £10,000.

Awards and scholarships are also given to CPE and PGDL students and pupillage trainees. Your application is restricted to one inn and early applications are recommended. Information is available from student officers at each of the Inns of Court.

ACCESS FUNDS

These are available for postgraduates experiencing particular difficulties in meeting living costs. (See General Access Funds and Hardship Funds under the Additional Support for Undergraduate Studies section of this chapter.)

SPONSORSHIP

A number of firms offer sponsorship for students taking vocational law courses. If you accept sponsorship you will usually be expected to serve your training contract with that firm. In some cases you will be expected to commit to a longer period of employment.

You should be able to find out more about sponsorship opportunities from your college careers service and in the CSU publication *Prospects Legal*. Twice a year *The Lawyer* magazine publishes a student special supplement with a list of sponsorship opportunities.

EDUCATIONAL CHARITIES AND TRUSTS

It isn't likely that a course lasting for more than one year could be financed entirely by trust fund help. However, educational charities and trusts can provide supplementary help to students who are without funding or who need additional help.

Charities usually pay one-off sums of up to around £300 for particular items or to make the difference between completion and non-completion of a course.

Some charities and trusts are quite precise in their requirements, restricting applications to people living in a particular area, or of a certain age, or with a parent working in a specific type of employment. For example, the Royal Scottish Corporation Training Grants are awarded to students in financial need who have lived within a 35 mile radius of Charing Cross, London for at least two years and are either Scottish born or are the child, spouse, widow or widower of someone born in Scotland.

As many charities and trusts work at a very local level it is worth starting with your local clergy, town hall or Citizens' Advice Bureau.

Advice on alternative sources of funding can be gained from the Educational Grants Advisory Service, (see Useful Addresses). Further information is to be found on the website www.scholar ship-search.org.uk.

MAKING A LITTLE GO A LONG WAY

As a student, offers of money will not be difficult to find. The generosity of companies offering you loans, overdrafts and credit cards can be overwhelming. At first it may appear that despite all the dire predictions of student poverty, you need never want for anything again.

At this point it's important to remember there is no such thing as a free lunch and the companies offering you money exist to make a profit, not to do you a favour.

Especially when you are undertaking a long course of study, such as qualfiying as a barrister or a solicitor, you need to start budgeting from the word go. A wild undergraduate year can make the difference between completing your studies and dropping out.

Many college student services, or National Union of Students (NUS) welfare services, offer money management and debt counselling services and these are well worth attending early on in your studies before matters get out of hand.

REALISTIC RESEARCH

If you've lived at home before going to university and relied on pocket money or the odd holiday job for money, a cheque for several thousand pounds can seem like an unending source of finance.

A recent survey revealed that around 50% of sixth-formers either underestimated or had no idea what their expenses would be at university.

The cost of living can vary enormously from area to area and if money is going to be tight, it's a good idea to look into local costs of accommodation and the availability of part-time work before you put in your application.

Also, make sure you're aware of your entitlements. And take advantage of discounts available to students through using your NUS card and www.nusonline.co.uk.

KEEP A NOTE OF WHAT YOU SPEND

You wouldn't be human if you've never put your card in a cash machine and been horrified at the small amount the unforgiving screen insists you possess.

However, for your own peace of mind you need to keep close tabs on where your money is going and what debts you have.

Before using your credit card to tide you over in difficult times, or before buying from a catalogue, check the interest rates and repayment conditions. Even a small slip from the repayment terms can bring severe penalties.

WHICH BANK WANTS MY OVERDRAFT THE MOST?

The answer is that at first sight all of them are fighting to offer you terms you just can't refuse. Cash refunds and retail discounts rank among the most common incentives you'll be offered to deposit your funds in a particular bank.

Don't be carried away by the generosity of these offers – take time to look at the small print. Check the interest rates for an account in credit and for an unauthorised overdraft. See if there is a branch near to your place of study and whether the branch has a student staff officer attached.

When embarking on legal training it's well worth checking a bank's graduate account arrangements, including preferential rates on loans and interest-free overdraft opportunities.

PART-TIME WORK

Research by the NUS revealed that 41% of students questioned
did part-time work during term-time. The average was 13 hours
of work a week and the average pay was £4.53 per hour. Many
students feel they have to take paid work in order to meet their
basic living costs.

If you know you will need to take part-time work in term-time to
support your studies, check whether the institutions to which you
are considering applying have employment agencies run by
student unions. If they do you may be guaranteed at least the
minimum wage. At the moment this is £3.60 an hour for 18–21
year olds and £4.20 for those over 22.

FURTHER INFORMATION

The NUS Welfare Unit produces a series of excellent information
sheets covering finance and other student related issues, (see
Useful Addresses).

PUBLICATIONS
A Guide for Individuals in Need, published by The Directory of
Social Change (DSC) – www.dsc.org.uk
Directory of Grant Making Trusts, published by the DSC
Charities Digest, published by Waterlows Legal Publishing
The Grants Register, published by Palgrave Macmillan Publishers
Ltd – www.palgrave.com

CHAPTER 12

Coping with the blips

*'The best laid schemes o' mice an' men
gang oft a-gley.'*

The words of the Scottish poet Robert Burns might have been written about legal training. Despite working hard, planning ahead and being as prudent as possible without joining the living dead, matters may not work out as you'd hoped.

How do you cope with the blips that arise and interfere with your plans?

It's important to remain positive and flexible and remember that, trite as it may sound, when one door closes another one has a habit of opening.

You have a law degree, but the future is less clear than it once was. It could be that:

● you don't have a place for the vocational stage of your training: either an LPC or BVC

- you've completed your BVC or LPC but haven't found a pupillage or training contract

- you've completed or will complete your law degree and you want to use your legal knowledge in your job, but you don't want to undertake further full-time training

- after gaining your degree you want a career that has nothing whatever to do with the law.

YOU HAVEN'T FOUND A PUPILLAGE OR A TRAINING CONTRACT

What are your options?

Having invested so much time, money and energy into getting where you are, the chances are the urge to continue is strong. Balanced against this is the fact that at this point unless you've won the lottery you're almost certainly running short of money.

YOU HAVEN'T BEEN OFFERED A PLACE ON A BVC OR LPC

In these situations you need to think carefully about why you've been unsuccessful so you can strengthen future applications. One thing that might be lacking is commercial legal experience.

In both cases you could consider the following:

PARALEGAL WORK
This involves working with a firm of solicitors on a short-term contract of possibly six months, supporting qualified staff in their work.

You bring to your job a great deal of legal knowledge, which makes you much more useful to the firm than somebody from a non-legal background. At the same time, you gain hands-on experience of legal work that looks good on your application forms.

As a paralegal you will be supervised and your work checked carefully by qualified staff, but you're likely to be given interesting tasks, such as assisting in background work, carrying out research, drafting legal documents and preparing material for trials.

Finding paralegal work with a firm is not likely to lead directly to a training contract, and some firms make a point of never offering training contracts to paralegal staff. What paralegal work does do is give you a chance to gain valuable practical experience and, most importantly, to see whether legal work is right for you.

Jo Rourke is a solicitor with a legal firm in London, specialising in entertainment law.

What does your job involve?
A lot of our clients are from the music industry and therefore a lot of our work is contract based. However, we do undertake a variety of other work, including litigation, which means I also go to court now and again.

The firm is quite small and the atmosphere in the office is relaxed and yes I do meet some famous faces.

How did you qualify?
I took a degree in European law with French and Spanish and then took a break for a couple of years. During that time I went travelling and took several jobs supposedly to save up for my LPC year, although that didn't quite work out.

Did you have trouble finding a training contract?
I started my LPC without one, which was a gamble, and I still didn't have one when I'd finished.

How did paralegal work help you?
After finishing my LPC, I took a paralegal job with a large city firm, working on a project in Bristol. The work lasted for ten months, at which point I took another paralegal job with my present firm.

> **When were you offered a training contract?**
> *After a few months. It was made clear at the interview that
> if we got on well there was a good chance the firm would
> take me on.*
>
> **Is it unusual for a paralegal job to lead to a training
> contract?**
> *It might be with the very big organisations, but I think it's
> something that often happens in smaller firms.*

YOU HAVE COMPLETED OR WILL COMPLETE YOUR LAW DEGREE

and are keen to use the knowledge you've gained but don't want
to embark on further full-time study.

You're not alone.

Fewer than 50% of law graduates enter full-time professional law
training courses. One of the major reasons for this is lack of
money. Unless you are receiving significant financial support from
your family, getting through the academic and postgraduate
stages of legal training is immensely difficult.

This means many individuals who would be an asset to the legal
profession opt for different careers, leaving the jobs for those who
are more financially secure, but no more talented. Both the Bar
Council and the Law Society have expressed concern over this
state of affairs.

ILEX

If you still want to train as a solicitor you could consider the ILEX
graduate option. Your legal degree will exempt you from all
examinations except for the legal practice examination. You will
then have to do five years' work under supervision before studying
part-time for your LPC, but you will get there and you will be
earning money and building up your client base during that time
(see Chapter 5).

PART-TIME BVC COURSES
The Inns of Court Law School and the BPP Law School both offer two-year part-time BVC courses.

PART-TIME AND DISTANCE LEARNING LPC AND GRADUATE DIPLOMA IN LAW CONVERSION COURSES
Combining part-time study with a full-time job is becoming an increasingly popular option. There are two main reasons for this. The first is that it avoids the massive debts that for most people are an inevitable part of full-time legal courses. The second is that it avoids periods of unemployment because students can remain in their existing employment while seeking a training contract or a pupillage.

Part-time courses include:

● traditional evening classes held twice a week

● Saturday classes held weekly

● weekend classes covering a Saturday and a Sunday every month

● distance learning.

The last two options are a good choice if you work long hours or evenings but they do demand more self-discipline than the other study options.

FUNDING A PART-TIME COURSE
Most part-time students pay their own fees and it is quite common for colleges to accept payment on a monthly instalment basis. Career Development Loans are also a possibility for part-time students (see Chapter 11).

A growing number of firms are offering sponsorship to part-time students so it's worth making contact with potential employers to see what they may offer.

If you're studying for a BVC, contact the Inns of Court to find out what support they can give you.

CHOOSING A PART-TIME COURSE
Before making a decision:

- Study college websites

- Attend open days

- Find out about the support given to part-time students and what books and other learning materials are provided on the course

- Remember it's helpful in planning your study schedule if you receive all the course materials at the beginning of your course

- Look at the experience a college has in running part-time legal courses

- Check whether the college has a specialist careers service and if it does what help it is likely to offer you

- Look for online facilities that could help you work from home or your office.

USING YOUR DEGREE IN LAW RELATED JOBS

You don't have to be a barrister or a lawyer to use your legal knowledge in work that brings you job satisfaction and career opportunities.

THE PRIVATE SECTOR
Many organisations have legal departments and employ people with a legal background. They range from major high street retailers to insurance companies and computer operations. The pay is usually good with these companies and you may find you enjoy the pace of work and the opportunities such jobs bring.

THE PUBLIC SECTOR
There are posts not only in the legal departments of county councils and district councils but also in other areas where there

is a need for legal knowledge, such as planning, social services and education departments.

Jobs in law and administration are available in local government and can lead to senior management posts.

Major utilities such as gas and electricity and their regulatory bodies have opportunities for law graduates.

Rachel Nixon is Executive Officer at the Ards Borough Council, Northern Ireland.

What does your job involve?
I support the town clerk and chief executive, carrying out research, preparing material for meetings, writing reports, studying and advising on the impact of proposed or actual legislation or other government policies on the council.

Are you a qualified solicitor?
No. I have a degree in European Law with Languages from the University of the West of England and I completed the Legal Practice Course at Nottingham Law School.

My original plan was to complete my legal training in England and then return to Northern Ireland, but I found it difficult to get a training contract in England and for that, and a number of other reasons, I decided to return home to Northern Ireland.

The training system is different there. Competition is extremely tough and I tried two years running to gain a place at the Institute of Professional Legal Studies without success.

What was your next step?
I joined Sainsbury's graduate management programme. After working in various stores I became a member of the retail systems team, introducing new IT systems into stores.

What brought you back into a law based job?
I was travelling a great deal between the UK and Northern Ireland, which was time consuming and not very mentally challenging. When I saw my present job advertised it specified a background in law and seemed to offer everything I wanted – responsibility, challenge, opportunities and the chance to live at home.

Do you regret not becoming a solicitor?
Not at all. I couldn't do my present job without my theoretical and practical experience.

I think it's important to realise there's far more to a legal career than being a solicitor or a barrister.

OTHER OPTIONS

● **Pressure groups and charities** take on staff with a legal background

● **Research** – the skills you have gained on a law degree, such as clear thinking, analytical strengths, plus your legal knowledge could make you a strong contender for this type of work

● **Teaching** – in recent years law has become a popular academic and vocational subject. You could look at taking a teaching qualification, or apply for a post teaching law

● **Law centres** – there are 61 centres in the UK providing free legal advice and representation. All of them employ some paid staff.

AFTER YOUR LAW DEGREE YOU WANT A CAREER THAT HAS NOTHING WHATEVER TO DO WITH LAW.

Read on. Chapter 13 is for you.

Non-legal options for law graduates

Whatever you decide to do at the end of your law degree course, you will take with you on graduation a range of practical, soft or transferable skills, which will be valuable whatever your future career choices may be.

These include:

- Communication skills – the ability to explain what you mean simply and clearly, both in speech and in writing

- Presentation skills – arranging information and putting it forward in an informative, interesting way

- Analytical skills – thinking through a problem logically in order to reach workable solutions

- Research skills – selecting information from reports, journals and books

- Team skills – the ability to work as part of a group

- Leadership skills – having the confidence to take the lead and take control of a situation

- Information technology skills – as with the majority of degree courses, law courses rely increasingly on the use of computers and computerised information.

Such skills make you highly attractive to employers in a wide range of employment sectors.

OTHER OPTIONS

FINANCE

This could be high on your list as the most popular choice among law graduates opting for a non-legal career is finance.

Major reasons for this are career opportunities and financial rewards. Successful graduates in the financial sector can earn immensely high salaries.

Employers look for a good degree in any subject plus numerical, analytical, communication and interpersonal skills.

ACCOUNTANCY

Professionally qualified accountants are known as either certified or chartered accountants. Their role is to make sure clients of whatever size make best use of their financial resources. They prepare and audit accounts, prepare tax returns, diagnose financial problems, give advice on mergers and corporate finance.

Accounting divides into two main areas: financial and management.

Training is provided by a number of professional bodies (see Useful Addresses), the largest being the ICAEW. Training consists of a three-year training contract with an authorised training firm, combining work experience with academic study and examinations.

Law graduates may apply for credit (to study to become an Associated Chartered Accountant with the ICAEW), providing they have completed the appropriate law modules as part of their studies. Law graduates (either single or joint honours) from the UK or the Republic of Ireland will automatically be awarded credit for both commercial and company law, providing a company law module has been completed.

BANKING

Many banks run accelerated or fast track programmes for graduates. The Bank of England runs a training scheme open to graduates with any degree, known as the Trainee Officials Programme.

Professional qualifications are awarded by the Institute of Financial Services (IFS), which is the official body of the Chartered Institute of Bankers (CIB) (see Useful Addresses).

INSURANCE

Insurance work falls into three main groups: life insurance, general insurance and commercial insurance. The professional body responsible for training in the insurance industry is the Chartered Insurance Institute (CII) (see Useful Addresses).

THE STOCK EXCHANGE

Market traders buy and sell shares. Before working as a market trader on the Stock Exchange it is necessary to pass the domestic equity market oral examination run by the Stock Exchange and the Securities Institute.

Stockbrokers are paid a commission by clients for advising them on investments on the Stock Exchange. Stockbrokers must be registered with the Financial Services Authority.

THE CIVIL SERVICE

Provides work for nearly half a million people and comprises over 170 departments and agencies. The Civil Service looks for quality recruits from every walk of life and legal graduates are often particularly well suited to a career in the Civil Service.

Vacancies are advertised on the Civil Service website, in the press and in professional journals.

THE CIVIL SERVICE FAST STREAM

Is the Civil Service accelerated development programme that offers a series of intensive job placements designed to prepare you for senior management positions.

EUROPEAN FAST STREAM

Aims to increase the number of British graduates securing permanent posts in EU institutions. It offers four years' training and work experience intended to improve chances of success in EU recruitment competitions. No particular language qualifications are required as these are developed during training.

EUROPEAN COMMISSION

Holds regular competitions for recruitment to its administrative grades and a legal background is seen as particularly useful.

ADMINISTRATION:

CHARTERED SECRETARY

Private and public companies are required by law to appoint a company secretary and many large organisations have company secretarial departments.

Chartered secretaries are employed as company secretaries and administrators in business, commerce, education, charities, investment trusts, hospitals and local authorities.

Graduates are exempt from the first part of the Institute of Chartered Secretaries and Administrators (ICSA) qualifying examinations. They have to complete the bridging programme modules covering financial accounting, corporate law, strategic and operations management and management accounting plus the professional programme modules of corporate governance, corporate secretaryship, corporate administration and corporate financial management.

Study is usually on a part-time basis while working in a relevant job. Around 70% of trainees have their fees paid by their employers. After three years' relevant work graduates can apply for associate membership and for fellowship after five years.

PERSONNEL OR HUMAN RESOURCES

This work involves recruiting the best people for the job and training and managing them to meet their full potential, thus making the organisation that employs them as efficient as possible.

Openings are to be found in a wide range of organisations, including department stores, supermarkets and factories, banks, health services, airlines, hotels, further and higher education institutes and travel companies.

The Chartered Institute of Personnel and Development (CIPD) considers law, together with degree subjects such as psychology and business studies, to be particularly suited to personnel work.

The professional qualification is the CIPD Professional Development Scheme involving around two years' part-time study usually while working in a personnel type job.

INFORMATION MANAGEMENT

Information managers work in public or academic libraries, in legal firms, medical organisations, scientific establishments, finance, industry, commerce, the media and wherever people need to access information. Graduates with a law degree plus a librarian/

information management qualification are in a good position to find work in a legal firm.

The Standing Conference of National and University Libraries (SCONUL) scheme enables graduates who are looking for a career in library and information management to spend a trainee year working in related employment in order to gain supervised experience of the work. Employers undertake to provide trainees with an overall view of the library system and experience of the day-to-day operation of a library.

After completing the trainee year, students can go on to a full-time course, or apply for a job and either study part-time for a professional qualification or delay further study for a time.

The Chartered Institute of Library and Information Professionals (CILIP) is the professional body for librarians and information managers or specialists (see Useful Addresses).

INFORMATION TECHNOLOGY

Around half of the graduates recruited to work in the IT industry do not have IT degrees.

The use of psychometric tests as part of the selection process is becoming more widespread because the tests give employers an idea of a candidate's ability to pick up new skills.

A graduate apprenticeship programme is available, with three key elements:

- An honours degree

- Key skills certificates

- Technical/optional units certificates selected to reflect the student's area of work.

See Useful Addresses for further information on information technology.

JOURNALISM

Graduates with degrees in any subject can make a career in journalism.

Seventy to eighty per cent of new entrants to journalism have taken a postgraduate course in journalism. Full-time courses recognised by the National Council for the Training of Journalists (NCTJ) or the Broadcast Journalism Training Council (BJTC) in various aspects of journalism are available at colleges in the UK and Northern Ireland. Part-time courses are also available.

There are still some opportunities for graduates to be recruited directly into jobs as journalism trainees on magazines and newspapers and as broadcast trainees by television companies.

PUBLISHING

The way into a career in publishing is often through a job as an editorial assistant with a publishing company.

There are postgraduate courses in publishing available at a number of universities and the Publishing Training Centre has a list of these (see Useful Addresses). However, the majority of graduates with degrees in all subjects get into publishing by taking whatever job they can.

SOCIAL WORK

Graduates who can show evidence of an interest in social work can apply to join a two-year postgraduate DipSW programme run at universities and colleges across the UK. Some bursaries are available to help with the financial cost of training and part-time courses are available so it is possible to have a job and gain a qualification at the same time (see Useful Addresses).

THE PROBATION SERVICE

Members of the Probation Service work in criminal courts giving advice on sentencing options, in prisons working with prisoners trying to change the attitudes that have led them to commit crimes and in the community with offenders who have been given rehabilitation and community punishment orders.

A degree in law together with subjects such as sociology and psychology are particularly suited to a career in the Probation Service.

Previous relevant work experience, usually in the form of voluntary work, is essential. Professional training leads to the Diploma in Probation Studies (DipPS). This two year training combines academic teaching and work-based supervised practice.

THE POLICE SERVICE

The service is looking for graduates with degrees in all subjects. Entry is by either the standard route or the High Potential Development Scheme. The latter aims to seek out the future leaders of the Police Service and to help them realise their potential through an individually tailored career development programme (see Useful Addresses).

CHAPTER 14

Retraining as a lawyer

THE LURE OF THE LAW

If you already have a job but your ambition is to retrain as a lawyer you could be joining a significant number of other people. Some use their existing professional experience to support their legal career, for example a surveyor might specialise in construction law, or a doctor in medical negligence cases.

THINK CAREFULLY

Retraining is a big step and you could be going back into student penury at a time when your friends are taking out mortgages and developing a taste for expensive food and holidays. Lifestyle differences can also put a strain on relationships.

If you are moving from a responsible professional position you could find starting at the bottom with a legal career very difficult.

On the plus side, after several years of full-time work your time management skills should be well developed and you should be

able to cope with a full-time postgraduate course without
difficulty.

PART-TIME STUDY

This certainly eases the financial burden of retraining although it
can make for some long days and nights. Law degrees are
available through part-time study and so are legal vocational
qualifications (see Chapter 5).

ACCESS COURSE IN LAW

If you're considering pursuing a legal career and you don't have
A-levels, as a mature student you could take an Access course in
Law.

The most popular method for mature entrants is by the ILEX route
(see Chapter 5).

FINDING TRAINING PLACES

Some firms actively welcome mature entrants because they bring
with them energy and commitment. However, some application
forms are geared to 21 year-olds. At 30+ you may find yourself
not only asked for your A-level grades but also to list positions of
responsibility held in the sixth form!

Amelia Gould is a trainee solicitor with Addleshaw
Goddard, a Manchester firm.

What was you first career?
I have an English degree and was a journalist.

What made you change to law?
My next step was either a move to London or retraining. I'd
studied a small amount of media law as a trainee journalist
and enjoyed it. Also, as a reporter I'd spent a lot of time at
the Crown Court and found it fascinating.

Was changing careers a big step?
In some ways it was enormous. I studied at Manchester Metropolitan University for my CPE and LPC so I didn't move house. I sold my car, which wasn't too drastic as the local transport system is good.

What was strange was suddenly having to count every penny. I worked as a legal secretary in the holidays, which was quite well paid, and I did some freelance journalism work, but it was still tough.

At what point did you find a training contract?
I applied for a couple before starting on the CPE course and did get second interviews, but at that point my knowledge of law was very limited and I wasn't offered a contract.

Between my CPE and LPC years I did a work placement with a legal firm and was offered a training contract. However, I opted for a training contract with my present firm. I had worked there as a legal secretary and been very impressed. I was given a training contract and sponsorship for my LPC year.

What is your advice to someone thinking of retraining?
Don't do it lightly. Get yourself some work experience and try to find some sponsorship.

The CPE and the LPC courses are fairly demanding, but if you're prepared to work then you should pass the courses without too much difficulty.

Useful addresses

LEGAL

INSTITUTIONS
The Bar Council
3 Bedford Row
London WC1R 4DB
Tel: 020 7691 8900
Website: www.barcouncil.org.uk

The Bar Council of Northern Ireland
Courts of Justice
91 Chichester Street
Belfast BT1 3JQ
Tel: 028 9056 2349
Website: www.barcouncil-ni-org.uk
Email: administration@barcouncil-ni.org.uk

Faculty of Advocates
11 Parliament House
Edinburgh EH1 1RF
Tel: 0131 226 5071
Website: www.advocates.org.uk

INNS OF COURT
Gray's Inn
8 South Square
London WC1R 5EU
Tel: 020 7458 7800
Website: www.graysinn.org.uk

Inner Temple
London EC4Y 7HL
Tel: 020 7797 8250
Website: www.inner
temple.org.uk

Lincoln's Inn
London WC2A 3LT
Tel: 020 7405 0138
Website: www.lincolnsinn.org.uk
Email: mail@lincolnsinn.org.uk

Middle Temple
2 Plowden Buildings
Temple
London EC4Y 9AT
Tel: 020 7429 4800
Website: www.middle
temple.org.uk
Email: members@middle
temple.org.uk

The Institute of Legal
Executives
Kempston Manor
Kempston
Bedford MK42 7AB
Tel: 01234 841000
Website: www.ilex.org.uk
Email: info@ilex.org.uk

The Institute of Professional
Legal Studies
10 Lennoxvale
Malone Road
Belfast BT9 5BY
Tel: 028 9033 5566
Website: www.qub.ac.uk/ipls
Email: p.rodway@qub.ac.uk

The Law Society
Ipsley Court
Berrington Close
Redditch B98 0TD
Tel: 020 7242 1222
Website: www.training.law
society.org.uk
Email: info.services@
lawsociety.org.uk

The Law Society of Northern
Ireland
Law Society House
98 Victoria Street
Belfast BT1 3JZ
Tel: 028 9023 1614
Website: www.lawsoc-ni.org
Email: info@lawsoc-ni.org

The Law Society of Scotland
26 Drumsheugh Gardens
Edinburgh EH3 7YR
Tel: 0131 226 7411
Website: www.lawscot.org.uk
Email: lawscot@lawscot.org.uk

The Legal Action Group
242 Pentonville Road
London N1 9UN
Tel: 020 7833 2931
Website: www.lag.org.uk
Email: lag@lag.org.uk

APPLICATIONS
LPC Central Applications Board
PO Box 84
Guildford
Surrey GU3 1YX
Tel: 01483 301282
Website: www.lawcabs.ac.uk

CPE Applications Board
PO Box 84
Guildford
Surrey GU3 1YX
Tel: 01483 451080
Website: www.lawcabs.ac.uk

RECRUITMENT
The Recruitment Branch
Crown Prosecution Service
50 Ludgate Hill
London EC4M 7EX
Tel: 020 7796 8053
Website: www.cps.gov.uk
Email: marianne.collins@
cps.gsi.gov.uk

The Recruitment Unit
The Scottish Executive
T Spur
Saughton House
Broomhouse Drive
Edinburgh EH11 3XD
Tel: 0131 244 3964
Website: www.scotland.gov.uk/
government/careers

GLS (Government Legal
Service) Recruitment Team
Queen Anne's Chambers
28 Broadway
London SW1H 9JS
Tel: 020 7210 3304
Website: www.gls.gov.uk
Email: recruit@gls.gsi.gov.uk

FUNDING

LOANS, GRANTS AND BURSARIES
HSBC
123 Chancery Lane
London WC2A 1QH
Tel: 0845 604 0626
Website: www.hsbc.co.uk
(Application forms available at
all branches – for specific
queries contact above address.)

Barclays Bank
Information line: 0800 400100
Website: www.barclays.co.uk

Royal Bank of Scotland
Application forms from
Commercial Banking Services
(Marketing)
PO Box 31
42 St Andrew Square
Edinburgh EH2 2YE
Tel: 0131 523 2631
Website: www.rbs.co.uk

The Educational Grants
Advisory Service (EGAS)
501–505 Kingsland Road
London E8 4AU
Tel: 020 7254 6251
Website: www.egasonline.org

National Union of Students
461 Holloway Road
London N7 6LJ
Tel: 020 7272 8900
Website: www.nusonline.co.uk
Email: nusuk@nus.org.uk

ACCOUNTANCY

The Association of Chartered
Certified Accountants
Student Promotions
29 Lincoln's Inn Fields
London WC2A 3EE
Tel: 020 7396 5700
Website: www.accaglobal.com

The Institute of Chartered
Accountants in England and
Wales
Gloucester House
399 Silbury Boulevard
Central Milton Keynes MK9 2HL
Tel: 01908 248108
Website: www.icaew.co.uk/
careers
Email: studentsupport@
icaew.co.uk

The Institute of Chartered
Accountants of Scotland
Student Education Department
C A House
21 Haymarket Yards
Edinburgh EH12 5BH
Tel: 0131 347 0100
Website: www.icas.org.uk
Email: enquiries@icas.org.uk

ADMINISTRATION

The Institute of Chartered
Secretaries and Administrators
16 Park Crescent
London W1B 1AH
Tel: 020 7580 4741
Website: www.icsa.org.uk
Email: info@icsa.co.uk

BANKING

The Institute of Financial
Services
IFS House
4–9 Burgate Lane
Canterbury
Kent CT1 2XJ
Tel: 01227 818609
Website: www.ifslearning.com
Email: customerservices@
ifslearning.com

The Chartered Institute of
Bankers of Scotland
Drumsheugh House
38B Drumsheugh Gardens
Edinburgh EH3 7SW
Tel: 0131 473 7777
Website: www.ciobs.org.uk
Email: info@ciobs.org.uk

CIVIL SERVICE

Capita RAS
Innovation Court
New Street
Basingstoke
Hampshire RG21 7JB
Tel: 01256 383780
Website: www.capitaras.co.uk
Email: ras.enquiries@
capita.co.uk

INFORMATION TECHNOLOGY

British Computer Society
1 Sanford Street
Swindon SN1 1HJ
Tel: 01793 417417
Website: www.bcs.org
Email: bcs hq@nq.bcs.org.uk

e-skills uk
1 Castle Lane
London SW1E 6DR
Tel: 020 7963 8920
Website: www.e-skills.com
Email: info@e-skills.com

INSURANCE

The British Insurance Brokers
Association
14 Bevis Marks
London EC3A 7NT
Tel: 020 7623 9043
Website: www.biba.org.uk
Email: enquiries@biba.org.uk

The Chartered Insurance
Institute
20 Aldermanbury
London EC2V 7HY
Tel: 020 7417 4793
Website: www.cii.co.uk
Email: customer.serv@cii.co.uk

JOURNALISM

Broadcast Journalism Training
Council
18 Millers Close
Ripingdale
Nr Bourne
Lincolnshire PE10 0TH
Tel: 01778 440025
Website: www.bjtc.org.uk
Email: secretary@bjtc.org.uk

National Council for the
Training of Journalists
Latton Bush Centre
Southern Way
Harlow
Essex CM18 7BL
Tel: 01279 430009
Website: www.nctj.com
Email: info@nctj.com

LIBRARY AND INFORMATION MANAGEMENT

Aslib The Association for
Information Management
Temple Chambers
3-7 Temple Avenue
London EC4Y 0HP
Tel: 020 7583 8900
Website: www.aslib.com
Email: aslib@aslib.com

CILIP
Chartered Institute of Library
and Information Professionals
7 Ridgmount Street
London WC1E 7AE
Tel: 020 7255 0500
Website: www.cilip.org.uk
Email: info@cilip.org.uk

PERSONNEL AND HUMAN RESOURCE MANAGEMENT

Chartered Institute of Personnel
and Development
CIPD House
35 Camp Road
Wimbledon
London SW19 4UX
Website: www.cipd.co.uk
Email: cipd@cipd.co.uk

POLICE

High Potential Development
Scheme
Fifth Floor Tower
Room 548
H M Inspectorate of
Constabulary, Personnel &
Administration
Home Office
50 Queen Anne's Gate
London SW1H 9AT
Tel: 020 7273 3000 or 0870 000
1585

The Scottish Police College
Tulliallan Castle
Kincardine
Alloa FK10 4BE
Tel: 0125 973 2000
Website: www.tulliallan.
police.uk
Email: it.support@tulliallan.
pnn.police.uk

The Police Service of Northern
Ireland
Brooklyn
65 Knock Road
Belfast BT5 6LE
Tel: 028 9065 0222
Website: www.psni.police.uk
Email: press@psni.police.uk

PROBATION SERVICE

National Association of
Probation Officers
3–4 Chivalry Road
Battersea
London SW11 1HT
Tel: 020 7223 4887
Website: www.napo.org.uk
Email: info@napo.org.uk

Probation Training Unit
Mitre House
231–237 Borough High Street
London SE1 1JD
Tel: 020 7740 8500
Website: www.probation-london.org.uk

PUBLISHING

The Publishing Training Centre
Book House
45 East Hill
Wandsworth
London SW18 2QZ
Tel: 020 8874 2718
Website: www.train4publishing.co.uk
Email: training@bookhouse.co.uk

London College of Printing
Elephant and Castle
London SE1 6SB
Tel: 020 7514 6514
Website: www.lcp.linst.ac.uk
Email: info@lcp.linst.ac.uk

SOCIAL WORK

Care Council for Wales
6th Floor
West Wing
Southgate House
Wood Street
Cardiff CF10 1EW
Tel: 029 2022 6257
Website: www.ccwales.org.uk
Email: info@ccwales.org.uk

General Social Care Council
Goldings House
2 Hays Lane
London SE1 2HB
Tel: 020 7397 5100
Website: www.socialwork careers.co.uk or www.gscc.org.uk

Northern Ireland Social Care
Council
7th Floor
Millennium House
19–25 Great Victoria Street
Belfast BT2 7AQ
Tel: 028 9041 7600
Website: www.niscc.info
Email: info@niscc.n-i.nhs.uk

Scottish Social Services Council
Compass House
11 Riverside Drive
Dundee DD1 4NY
Tel: 0845 603 0891
Website: www.sssc.uk.com
Email: enquiries@sssc.uk.com

THE STOCK EXCHANGE

Financial Services Authority
25 The North Colonnade
Canary Wharf
London E14 5HS
Tel: 020 7066 1000
Website: www.fsa.gov.uk
Email: enquiries@fsa.gov.uk

Publicity Information Department
The London Stock Exchange
Old Broad Street
London EC2N 1HP
Tel: 020 7797 1000
Website: www.londonstock
exchange.com
Email: enquiries@londonstock
exchange.com